Foreword by Jack Hayford

To Heaven & Back

True Stories

of Those Who

Have Made

the Journey

Rita Bennett

ZONDERVAN™

GRAND RAPIDS, MICHIGAN 49530 USA

ZONDERVAN™

To Heaven and Back
Copyright © 1997 by Rita Bennett

Requests for information should be addressed to:
Zondervan, *Grand Rapids, Michigan 49530*

Library of Congress Cataloging-in-Publication Data

Bennett, Rita
    To heaven and back : true stories of those who have made the journey / Rita
Bennett.
      p. cm.
    Includes bibliographical references.
    ISBN 0-310-21078-X
    1. 1. Near-death experiences—Christianity.   I. Title.
BT833.B36 1997
236'.1—dc21
                                          97-14381

Interior design by Sue Vandenberg Koppenol

Printed in the United States of America

03 04 05 06 07 08 09 /❖ DC/ 21 20 19 18 17 16 15 14 13 12 11 10

This book is lovingly dedicated to God the Father,
my Abba;
to Jesus the Son, my Savior;
and to the enabling Holy Spirit, my inspirer.
May Jesus, Light of the World and Light of Heaven,
light up our lives now and forever.

To Daye —
May Heaven touch
you as you read.
Lovingly,
Rita Bennett
5-1-03

Contents

Acknowledgments

Many people have been like candles to light my way in writing this book on heaven. Seven candles of hope are Valvita Jones, Deborah O'Donnell, Gerard Landry (and Denise), Carolyn McCormick, Pam Johnstone, Lorraine Tutmarc, and Craig Gottschalk. You willingly shared your "to heaven and back" experiences with me and now with the world. Please accept my heartfelt gratitude for your entrusting me with your heavenly treasures. May you receive many rewards from God in this life and eventually on your return trip Home. Lorraine already has.

One special candle who shed much light in my life and in our world before his one-way journey home is my beloved husband, Dennis. His departure caused me to want to learn more about heaven and is a major reason for my writing this book.

A light of encouragement is Judy Brown, the first person to read chapters 1 through 9, which helped her on her journey. She in turn helped me with her excellent feedback. I am thankful for her amazing encouragement to me while she was dying. At that time neither of us knew her story would be in chapter 14.

One light of wisdom is Dr. Amos Daniel Millard, my new friend and special gift during the writing of part 3. We had many discussions on biblical history of the Jews and their homeland, though some of that material will be used in other writings. Amos has been like a personal professor to me. He is presently a retired professor of Biblical Archaeology at Northwest College, Kirkland, Washington.

Three candles of Jewish wisdom are Dr. Dick and Polly Perkins, who shared their knowledge of Jewish history, and Zola Levitt, who inspired me with his television program and teaching on the Jewish wedding.

Four lights of caring are Dr. Keith and Lee Oles, who recommended the story of their friend Deborah O'Donnell for the book

7

and also gave me consistent encouragement for many years; my brother, Bill Reed, who sent me Gerard Landry's personal testimony in my time of need (what a surprise to both of us that it would become part of this book!); two other caring sibling lights, Bob Reed and Georgia Reed Danahy; and Betty Bell, who helpfully did research in locating near-death experiencer Valvita Jones.

Many intercessory candles who were continually committed to praying for me include Betty Bell, Joy Bennett, Judy Dupre-Gervais, Robert and Lucy Ervin, Helen Gawel, Liz Glover, the Rev. Don Goodheart, Barbara Gornell, Bob and Susan Hayes, Anne King, Vesta Lerdrup, Ray and Daphne McGregory, Gary and Joy McLaury, Richard and Gloria Melchior, the Rev. Ted and Lee Ann Nelson, the Rev. Dick and Shade O'Driscoll, Erline Reber, Gladys Rogers, John and Jean Rosling, Ruth Salama, Kay Strong, Betty Tapscott, Jim and Sheila Todd, Nancy Tyler, Margaret Welch, Shirley Wilson, Dorothy Wright, and Anita Zinter.

Helping lights include Lisa Schweiter, Christian Renewal Association volunteer, for counting and evaluating, via *Cruden's Concordance*, the times *heaven* is found in the Bible; Beth Hubbard, who checked on several reference books for me; Dianne Herivel and Shirley Wilson, who listened and responded to my list of chapter opening quotes; and Maxie Cissna, Linda James, and Patty Pearson, who helped at CRA.

A faithful candle is my secretary, Gigi Esnough. I am thankful for her assistance in many things: calling the library with my questions, answering the phone, putting up with my odd writing hours, talking on the intercom though not seeing me for days at a time.

Many writers' lights must be recognized: Paul Sinor, author and college professor, who spoke to the Edmonds North by Northwest Writers and gave me timely tips; the members of North by Northwest Writers, who gave me book title suggestions and encouragement during my "labor pains"; and new writing friend, Monica Coglas, who reminded me to use "romance bookends."

Research candles include Marsha Ford of *Charisma* magazine, who helped locate magazine articles on both Olympic winners and Christian martyrs; Janet Biggart, who also assisted in locating an Olympic winners article; and the Edmonds Public Library, which unearthed numerous books and other information for me. Special thanks to Evie at the reference desk. I also want to thank the Seattle Public Library, downtown, for always being cooperative and helpful.

Topping off the light is Zondervan's great editorial team, the best I've worked with in my writing career: Ann Spangler, Evelyn Bence, and Mary McNeil. I am thankful for their believing in me, for their consistent wise choices, and for their bringing out the best. They are a gift from heaven to me. Thanks also to the others on Zondervan's staff who worked behind the scenes.

As you can see from this list, it takes many people to write a book. Grateful thanks to you, one and all.

And it takes you, the reader, to find and read the book. I want to thank you, my friend, for coming with me on this journey to heaven and back. May your light shine a little brighter on your return when you finish the last page, and then may you hold the light high for others to find their way.

Foreword

Forewords to books are requested by authors and publishers who think there is some constituency that may be interested in what the writer of the foreword has to say. It's encouraging, if not flattering, to be asked—even if that constituency only exists in the author's and publisher's minds! But if, indeed, there is someone reading this because they wonder about my thoughts relative to this book, here is my primary one: *Caution! Read the label first!*

I don't say this because I have reservations. I say it because you deserve to know in advance the distinct values that have governed the preparation of this needed study.

This is more than an inspiring book, it is an insightful one. And best of all, its insights are not of the mysical, arcane, or cultish variety that are in such proliferation right now. Instead, you're about to enter the pages of a book written by a clear-thinking, insistent-on-truth's-hard-facts woman—a person of pragmatic intellect who also happens to be remarkably loving, humanly sensitive, and gently compassionate. If you "read the label first" you'll discover this immediately.

This "label" to which I refer is part 1 on this book. Rita Bennett clears the debris from the broad terrain of present-day attitudes and reports regarding "near-death experiences." She writes in exactly the same good-sense style that she did with her late husband, Dennis, enriching multitudes as they shared so effectively in teaching and counseling, as well as writing. The solid and balanced mix of sound intellectual processing, joined to sensitive spiritual insights rooted in divine revelation, is both assuring and gratifying to the thoughtful reader. But there's even more.

There's a commitment to caution—that neither too much nor too little be drawn from a study such as this. Today, too few inquirers into the subject matter of death, heaven, hell, and the "tunnel" from this life to the next are sufficiently schooled to be cautious. Too many, with an abandon born either of curiosity—or more

often a need for comfort regarding the death of a loved one—
absorb reports, books, and other literature that overstep God's
wisely given boundaries. Desperate in their search for hope and
wandering in a desert of loneliness, sincere souls chase mirages or
drink at poisoned pools. I think Mrs. Bennett has set appropriate
perimeters in place and thereby mapped some unfamiliar terrain
in a way that offers us a beautiful yet discerning look into a subject deserving of so gracious-yet-cautious an approach.

There's one more thing . . .

I want to commend both Rita and the people at Zondervan
for their willingness to take the risk involved in this work. Both
parties are already renowned for their commitment to the abiding
values that are garnered from keeping all life's (and death's) issues
rooted in God's holy Word. Yet they have chosen to take the risk of
enduring the small-souled criticism of the sure-to-be-heard-from
handful of pretending "purists" who will assail this effort. I regret
that they will face that, but I want to pay tribute to those who
embrace the larger vision and have willingly taken the challenge.

A host of hungry, grieving, and searching souls are needful of
the comfort available through such a compassionate resource as
this. An even larger number of interested inquirers, surrounded by
the plethora of published NDE reports in our day, deserve so sensi-
ble and spiritually sensitive a presentation. My pastoral heart for the
hurting is pleased to be able to tell people about this book, but for
one primary reason: My pastoral passion for biblical balance is
assured; those who read these pages will be guarded against cultish
confusion and kept pointed along a pathway of spiritual safety.

So, now, please, "read the label." And proceed to be enriched
by the interesting, insight-filled, and comforting message of *To
Heaven and Back*. The book is trustworthy because the author is.
The book is also truth-filled—because of another Author. He's the
One who first came from heaven that He might take back any of us
who want to go—back to the Father's heart, in love . . . back to the
Father's home, forever.

His Name is Jesus,

Jack W. Hayford, D. Litt., Senior Pastor
The Church On The Way, Van Nuys, California

A Word from a Physician

In this book, Rita Bennett takes her readers on a trip to the great beyond and back again to earthly life. She suggests that you and I stop for a moment and accept that another day we will make this trip to eternity one way. With that thought in mind, we can all profit from quiet contemplation of what Rita is telling us.

The near-death experiences that she recounts of those who have departed and returned tell us of adventure in the highest sense. We need to reflect on these lessons and free ourselves from undue attachments to this life, so that we can properly prepare for the next.

Rita teaches us to love life to the fullest in a spiritual sense and, at the same time, to anticipate the infinite joys of heaven for all eternity. She tells us to put our faith in Christ and be joyful. We are not to worry, for God will take care of us and, when ready, He will call us home.

This powerful book calls us to accept God as our Savior and to regard life here as an opportunity to do His work on earth. By doing for others out of love, we will become happier than we have ever been.

As a heart surgeon who has operated on thousands of patients, I've seen many, many lives changed spiritually for the better. This is a book I would be happy to share with my patients, and I highly recommend it to you, the reader.

The overriding message of *To Heaven and Back* is that God is real and that we can join our Lord for all eternity if we put Christ first in our lives. If we do, He will reward us for a life well lived. More than that we cannot ask.

Lester R. Sauvage, M.D.
Founder and Medical Director
The Hope Heart Institute

PART ONE

*Let It Be
for
Healing*

CHAPTER ONE

Looking for Answers

*Forgiveness is a touch of heaven, heals the wounded heart,
and leads to heaven.*

Rita Reed Bennett

———◆———

"The most wonderful experience in my life resulted from one of the worst experiences I've ever had," said Margo to her customer. "My husband hit me on the head with a hammer, and I fell to the floor, unconscious, with a fractured skull. But what happened next changed me forever. I had a near-death experience."

Listening in shock and awe, I stood in a check-out line twenty-five years ago, hearing for the first time a story of a person who believed she had died, gone to heaven, and come back. Margo (not her real name) was the manager of a small store in Seattle. I thought, *What woman in her right mind would speak like this unless she truly had a transforming experience? How could something so good come out of something so bad?*

Remarkable as it sounds, Margo's near-death experience (NDE) healed her memories of brutality, took away bitterness, gave her a positive attitude, made her an encourager to others in distress, and gave her a new sense of hope for the future. It is hard to ignore or devalue such benefits. That is what makes this, and the more detailed stories of such experiences as told in part 2 of this book, so intriguing.

What about you? Something must have prompted you to pick up this book. Has a magazine article, a book, or a TV special on near-death experiences piqued your interest? Have you yourself had such an experience, or do you know someone who has? Perhaps you have grieved the loss of a loved one and that experience has led you to seek answers.

As a result of advancements in resuscitation techniques, more and more people are coming back from the brink of death. In 1989 it was estimated that sixteen million people worldwide were in this category.[1] Subsequently, according to a Gallup poll "at least eight million people in America alone have had near-death experiences."[2] In another study, more than five hundred personally interviewed people shared their NDEs.[3]

What Is a Near-Death Experience?

Many in the field of medicine acknowledge a physical state called "near death," in which one's heart can be stopped for up to four minutes (up to twenty-five minutes or more on rare occasions, such as drowning or lightning strike).[4] At times one can "return" to life from being dead or at the brink of death. Not everyone who is near death has a near-death *experience*, as defined below. And not everyone who glimpses heaven has proof of his or her heart stopping.

What is a *near-death experience*? An NDE is when a person nearly dies or dies and comes back (often by resuscitation), having had varying degrees of supernatural experience from small to full-blown. Dr. Melvin Morse, in his book *Transformed by the Light*, gives nine traits of an NDE. As one physically hangs in the balance between life and death, one (1) has a sense of being dead, (2) has a sense of peace and painlessness, (3) has an out-of-body experience, (4) has a tunnel experience, (5) sees people of light—often relatives or friends, (6) sees a being of light, often thought to be Jesus or an angel, (7) experiences a life review, (8) is reluctant to return, and (9) experiences personality transformation upon return. He says, "To have all nine traits is to experience a 'full-blown' NDE. Those are rare."[5] Apparently even a few of these traits can be a transforming experience. I would add a tenth trait: (10) a decreased fear of death. (See the statistics of Dr. Michael Sabom in chapter 4.)

Stephen Miller wrote an interesting and balanced article entitled "Back from the Brink" for *Physician* magazine, a Focus on the

Family publication. Miller quotes Alex Deasley, professor of New Testament at Nazarene Theological Seminary in Kansas City: "Some NDEs are clearly the work of God," he says. "The curtain between this world and the next is pulled back by God for the reassurance of His people in distress." Miller also quotes Dr. David Hager, an obstetrician/gynecologist from Lexington, Kentucky: "I think it's a drawing near of God's presence in our lives to reassure us and to help us through the fear of that transition [death]."[6]

In this book I measure the validity of NDEs in terms of the ten essential traits noted above. The people whose stories I include physically stood on the brink of death—due to serious illness, physical trauma, or accident. Such condition caused the human spirit to separate from the body long enough to have an encounter with heavenly beings or heaven itself before returning. Whether the experience lasted seconds or minutes is not crucial to discern; much can happen in the final microseconds of a person's life as he or she enters into eternity's realm of timelessness.

In the accounts that follow, when the person knows how long his or her heart stopped, I have clearly stated so. Most experiences related in part 2 took place in hospitals and one under medical observation at home. Two of the seven occurred when the person was at home and unattended. In all of these experiences I see evidence of quite a number of the ten traits for NDEs.

Controversy

Controversies are brewing over the topic of near-death experiences. A number of books about NDEs have been published, and the stories retold in many of today's best-selling titles mainly have to do with a positive experience of seeing a light; a heavenly sphere; and often a person recognized as Jesus Christ, an angel, or a deceased loved one. Relatively few stories about dark experiences have surfaced. People whose faith is not grounded in biblical revelation but who have had positive NDEs usually feel all who die will have the same positive experience, and they usually are no longer afraid of their own death nor of anyone else's.

Understandably, Christians are worried about positive reports of *unbelievers* who nearly die and come back as unbelievers still. They are afraid that such experiences will lull the NDEer to sleep spiritually, and when that person dies he or she will be lost forever to God's loving presence.

A close look at NDEs reveals that many people don't get very far into the heavenly realm before they are sent back to earth. We don't know what spiritual battles would have followed had they stayed longer and tried to enter heaven. Even when the great leader Moses died, God and Satan were in battle over his body (Deut. 34:5–6; Jude 9). This last battle must not be taken lightly by any of us.

Examples in the chapters that follow show the kinds of battles that can take place near the end. As you read, you will find that Lorraine Tutmarc and Craig Gottschalk were on the outskirts of hell and were saved from destruction literally "by the skin of their teeth." I don't know whether you believe in heaven or hell, and my purpose here is not to debate who will go to either place. God alone is judge of that. However, to be complacent about the end of life is the worst decision that could be made.

Five Views of NDEs

Near-death experiences are among the most thought-provoking mysteries of life. Most everyone is trying to figure them out. In my research for this book, I read most of the recent books in print as well as a number of biblically oriented books written in the seventies. We can categorize these books into five groups (this book lies in the fifth category) based on how each genre addresses the issue of near-death experiences.

1. Scientific Category

Some authors try to figure out NDEs scientifically. Most don't believe in a life after death, but some are not closed to the possibility.

Many doctors and scientists are trying to figure out what causes near-death experiences. Renowned pediatrician Dr. Melvin Morse wrote *Closer to the Light*, a book in which he gives accounts of children who have died and come back. Unfortunately, at the end of his book, he explains the positive experiences of seeing light, Jesus, angels, and departed relatives as simply the effects of endorphins having been released by the brain to help people through this difficult death passage. After one's happy departure through a tunnel of light, one ceases to exist.

Dr. Morse says, "I am often told by those who've had these experiences that they resent my attempt to localize NDEs in the brain. To them, attempting to scientifically explain these events is the same as attempting to debunk them, to imply that they are not real."[7] Morse tries to keep an open mind by concluding, "Whether or not there is some part of man that can leave the physical body is for each person to decide for himself."[8]

Morse and some other researchers think that most elements of the NDE come from the brain's right temporal lobe located in the area above the ear. In his second book, *Transformed by the Light,* Morse calls this area the "circuit board of mysticism."[9] One thing Morse admits he can't pin down and localize in the physical brain is the light people claim to see. He states, "I do believe that the light seen by NDEers comes from a source outside the body."[10]

Dr. Michael Sabom, a cardiologist and professor at Emory University School of Medicine, gives a different scientific conclusion. His book *Recollections of Death* discusses findings of his five-year study of seventy-eight patients who had nearly died (of these, thirty-three had NDEs). He leans toward the opinion that our being may consist of two fundamental elements, a "mind" and a "brain." He acknowledges that this is in contrast to the Western scientific thought that is "firmly molded around the premise that all aspects of human consciousness—our total being—can be or eventually will be explained through the physiologic interaction of the cellular components of the human brain."[11] Sabom quotes Sir Charles Sherrington, Nobel laureate in medicine in the thirties, and Wilder Penfield, a neurosurgeon and researcher of the brain, to confirm his own view of the dualistic (mind and brain) system. "These theories, proposed by Sherrington, Penfield and others at least establish a framework in which to consider the NDE as a possible 'out of body' event: a mind-brain split."[12]

The theory of the mind and brain being two parts within the human person allows scientific thought to concede that life may go on after death. As defined by Webster's dictionary, *mind* can be used interchangeably with *soul*; the mind is the element that "feels, perceives, thinks, wills, and especially reasons."[13] Sabom's book is well written, has an intellectual scientific approach, and gives hope for more than a physical existence.

2. Agnostic and Atheist Category

Some agnostics and atheists seem to need to disprove NDEs to maintain their belief systems. They are concerned about this increasing phenomenon and the stories of supernatural experiences.

British psychologist and parapsychology researcher Susan Blackmore articulates the antisupernaturalist viewpoint: "NDEs, mystical experiences and everything encountered on the spiritual path are products of a brain and the universe of which it is a part. For there is nothing else."[14] Many similarly minded researchers would evaluate NDEs as strictly psychological phenomena put in terms of the dying person's cultural expectations.

In response to the worldview of Blackmore and others, I quote Dr. Howard Dueker, a brain surgeon. Before his death, I visited him in his home. We discussed the brain and the scientific theory that humans are simply animals with highly evolved brains. Dueker countered that concept with a wise statement: "The brain is not the soul, but the machinery of the soul."[15] He further explained that, to his view, at death the "soul machinery" dies but the human soul does not.

Following Dueker's line of thinking, NDEs may be processed in the brain, specifically in the right temporal lobe, but that doesn't mean they (or other supernatural experiences) are limited to the human body.

3. Nonreligious, Nonbiblical Supernatural Category

The greatest number of books about NDEs today are written by authors studying specific NDEs—their own or others'—and interpreting them through occultic belief systems. These people and their readers are curious about the supernatural, are open to the mystical, and they explore nonbiblical interpretations of NDEs.

Many such people are spiritually hungry and looking for answers. To them, most any spiritual experience is acceptable, including the occult. Those who are not alive in spirit and soul through Christ, however, are not able to understand or properly evaluate NDEs or any supernatural experiences. Being spiritually hungry and vulnerable, they often confuse darkness for light.

Moving into the supernatural can be particularly dangerous without the inner compass of the indwelling Spirit of God or the outer compass of biblical wisdom. Unaware of the danger, some promote occult teachings of communication with the "dead," reincarnation, spiritism (now called channeling), fortune telling, magic, and other experiences against which the Bible gives severe warnings.[16] People involved in these or other related practices are in spiritual bondage, having removed themselves from God's protection.

For spiritually hungry seekers, the safe supernatural avenue is available through the new-birth experience as described in the Bible (John 3:3–16; Acts 2:17–18). This spiritual birth is even more transforming than a near-death experience. (It may be accompanied by visions, dreams, impartations of knowledge, and other supernatural gifts. In an earlier book I addressed the important issue of spiritual empowerment.)[17] Those who move in the supernatural are safe only if they follow the path set down in the Bible. This warning is not meant to turn away seekers but to lovingly invite you to come along with me and explore a better way to direct your spiritual quest.

4. Christian Cessationist Viewpoint

A number of books have been written by Christians who are so afraid of the excesses that they believe most NDEs are tricks of the netherworld to lead people into destructive occult practices. Some new books in this category are a backlash against books slanted toward the occult.

Cessationist Christians feel that we live in an age in which all valid supernatural experiences, except salvation, have ceased; this means that they theologically put NDEs in the occult realm. Reg Grant, professor of pastoral ministries at Dallas Theological

Seminary, says, "Most NDEs are either organic and devoid of spiritual significance or else they're satanic."[18]

Such attitudes can cause people who have had legitimate NDEs to withdraw and be afraid to share their experiences with the church. Yes, some people have entered into cults or the occult after an NDE, but that does not mean that critics are correct when they claim that most NDEs are occultic.

Such polarized views create more problems than they solve. How many people have had NDEs and then looked to the church for answers? Christians and other seekers have had little solid Christian leadership to guide them after their experiences. How many have strayed into the occult because the church has failed to take leadership in addressing this important issue? In this vacuum, people have turned to occult or cultic explanations and guidance. If biblically sound ministers, doctors, and other leaders don't get involved, many innocent people will be misled.

One needs to be careful of condemning virtually all NDEers lest one unnecessarily wound Christians who have had valid NDEs. I know of one young woman who was going to tell her story on TV but had second thoughts when her concerned parents and friends warned her that some Christians would likely identify her with the occult. Out of fear, she canceled her plans. Promotion of condemnation and fear is not the answer.

5. *Christians Seeking God's Truth*

Some Christians have written scripturally based accounts, or testimonies, of their own or others' NDEs in an effort to comfort readers mourning the death of loved ones.

Genuinely concerned Christians want to know the truth about NDEs within a scriptural framework and are willing to consider whether valid testimonies can draw them closer to God, giving them and their loved ones a glimpse of the afterlife. They have a solid biblical foundation that allows them to sift the stories and separate the valid from the invalid. I think, for example, of Rexella Van Impe, nationally known television personality, a beautiful Christian who had a near-death experience and then continued to be biblically sound in her teaching and commentating. Such Christians are willing to stand for the truth and resist polarization. They want to listen to, receive inspiration from, offer guidance to, and affirm others who have had an NDE. They are encouraged to see how God is using the modern medical breakthrough of resuscitation to help his children, sometimes even giving them a glimpse of heaven.

My hope is that, by offering biblically sound guidelines by which to judge NDEs, this book, which fits in this fifth category, will lend balance to the understanding of NDEs in Christian circles. I will also give an exciting picture of the afterlife. To my knowledge this is the first book that includes positive, detailed accounts of NDEs *and* an in-depth biblical picture of heaven.

Lay Controversies Aside

Christians can be polarized worse than Democrats and Republicans. Because of the mixture of truth and error in some NDE writings, some Christians don't want to read or hear any near-death testimonies and are determined to stop others from hearing them. Their premise is that most NDEs are occultic, so why pay any attention to them? And besides, the Bible tells us all we need to know about heaven.

It is true that God's Word is the instruction book for life and death. That is foundational, of course. However, since the church welcomes testimonies about other life experiences, why shouldn't we hear from those who have had a touch of heaven? Can't we be trusted to use Scripture to evaluate the message, just as we do for other attempts at witnessing? I personally have been helped by contemporary witnesses who confirm that what Scripture teaches is true.

Attending high school in the warm clime of Florida, I read about the snowy land of Alaska and its Eskimo population. But my book knowledge took on new significance in 1966, when my husband and I actually visited the far northern village of Point Hope, Alaska, from which one can look across the Chukchi Sea and see Russia. Meeting the Alaskan people and seeing the terrain did not invalidate my geography book but made it all the more real to me.

Is there biblical evidence for the validity of NDEs? It seems as though the apostle Paul may have had a near-death experience when religious leaders from Antioch incited a crowd at Lycaonia to stone Paul. They took him outside the city and threw him in the rubbish and left him for dead. Scripture says, "However, when the disciples gathered around him, he rose up" (Acts 14:20 NKJV). The Greek word *anistemi*, meaning to stand up or rise again, is used here and 110 other times in the Bible, forty times when speaking of the resurrection.[19] This goes far in confirming Paul's death and return, a kind of resurrection, which may well have come about through the disciples' prayers.

By our present definitions, Paul may well have had a full-blown NDE. Paul later humbly gives this witness: "And I know such a man—whether in the body or out of the body I do not know, God knows—how he was caught up into Paradise [a biblical term for heaven] and heard inexpressible words, which it is not lawful for a man to utter" (2 Cor. 12:3–4 NKJV). Paul then talks about how God had to deal with him so he would not be exalted and prideful about this experience.

Paul didn't want to be carried away by any revelations he had experienced; this is a good word of caution to an NDEer or anyone else who has received a supernatural revelation. And those who hear such testimonies need to be careful not to be too awed by the person who claims to have talked to Jesus personally and then been sent back. I was encouraged by the first person who shared her NDE with me, and I continue to be encouraged by others. Though someone may have had one of the greatest adventures imaginable, we need to remember that he or she is just as human and prone to sin and error as any of us.

Having an NDE may open a person up physically and mentally to the spiritual world. This is why more than ever that person needs the church's help and guidance. After the "return" an experiencer may be more susceptible to either blessings or deception. (Carolyn McCormick talks about this in chapter 6.) We mustn't condemn experiencers or try to destroy a message that God has sent to heal and comfort the bereaved or to help someone preparing for his or her own departure. Rather, we should encourage valid experiencers and be inspired by them.

Good and Bad Books

At the end of this book I provide a recommended reading list of books that are inspirational and theologically and spiritually sound. Such books will encourage bereaved Christians working through their grief. Books that would lead a person into spiritism,[20] the occult (often called the New Age), or loss of faith are not included in the list.[21] Nor did I list books that I saw as being elaborations of NDEs with extensive "messages" of the person's own belief system. I appreciate books that tell exactly what happened in a person's NDE and nothing more. As with the proverbial fish story, it is easy to build on to what happened. Writing an entire book on an experience that lasted only minutes could tempt a person to pad a bit.

Also excluded from the reading list are books that condemn or invalidate all supernatural NDEs. If your favorite book on NDEs is not on the list, it may be for one of the above-mentioned reasons or because it is out of print or too recent.

The NDE experiences given in this book reflect God's Word; they are not a substitute for it or an addition to it. My book is in no way intended to develop a religion from those resuscitated or recalled from the dead. It is not proposing, as some have coined NDE testimonials, a "religion of the resuscitated," but reaffirming the truth of the gospel that leads to a life-saving relationship with the resurrected Lord. I agree with this excellent statement by Douglas Groothuis: "We should dismiss the 'religion of the resuscitated' and instead embrace the eternal certainties offered by the One who experienced death, burial, resurrection, and ascension to the place of unmatched authority. He alone has the last word on matters of life and death."[22]

Groups Meeting to Share NDEs

In many cities NDEers meet together in support groups to discuss their experiences. People who have had NDEs often feel different from others and are afraid to talk about their experiences for fear of ridicule or ostracism. Some people turn to these NDE meetings as a substitute for church; here they feel more acceptance, love, and even more of the supernatural than they sense in some church services. The group meetings are usually inspiring. People tell their own stories, often without giving any spiritual conclusions, and the hearers draw the stories through their own spiritual screens. The group generally does not "judge" others' NDEs. By sharing their stories in this setting, many experiencers receive emotional comfort, lessening their feelings of isolation.

Since these are public meetings, it is understandable that the leaders don't want to favor one particular faith. Considering the inclusive nature of these groups and their lack of Christian discernment, I strongly advise that anyone attending such a group be grounded in Scripture and covered by prayer, while exhibiting the gracious, reconciling love of Christ.

NDEers may well be turning to support groups because the church is not providing answers for their experiences. If the church itself doesn't see the value of allowing people to tell their stories and of helping them, many who are seeking answers will get in spiritual trouble. We have an opportunity to make a contribution if we are willing and not hypercritical. More churches should be open to such inspiring testimonies, and some might go a step further and provide support groups for NDEers and those who are grieving.

Let It Be for Healing

I have brought up the controversies of which I am aware so that we can look at them and deal with them. This is not a book advocating wholesale acceptance of NDEs, nor is it a book of wholesale rejection of NDEs. It is a book using God's Word and Spirit as the plumb line of what to accept. *To Heaven and Back* will help you be better able to discern what is valid and what is not as you read other materials. If you do not agree on every point, please read the whole book to see if your question is answered later. God has gifts that he would like to give you; don't let anything hinder your receiving them. Having looked at the challenges, let the rest of this book be for healing.

This book's main purpose is to give people hope and a glimpse of heaven. It is to comfort the bereaved and to prepare the dying for the next life. And by the "next life," I don't mean a different one. It is a continuation of the same one but in a dimension outside time and into eternity, beyond anything we have known on earth. Hope for the next life helps us to live more loving lives with greater purpose now and later.

My desire is that by reading this book you will be more prepared for this life, for your departure—whether by death or when Christ returns to catch away his people[23]—and for the life hereafter. Come. Let's walk along together in the atmosphere of heaven. Don't be afraid. Jesus will weep with you, will comfort you, and eventually will wipe the tears from your eyes—all things in his time.

PART TWO

*Let It Be
for Love*

CHAPTER TWO

Let Heaven Heal You

Hope is like the sun, which, as we journey towards it, casts the shadow of our burden behind us.

Samuel Smiles
Self Help

Has life dealt you pain that you're having trouble coping with? Is your own pain almost more than you can bear? Or are you finding it difficult to watch those around you who are struggling with life's physical challenges? Remember the wise, true words of hymn writer Thomas Moore: "Earth has no sorrow that heaven cannot heal."

Heaven can heal your sorrow. It has healed mine. Here I will briefly recount the deepest sorrow of my life, the sorrow that drew me to a new awareness of heaven, my home above.

November 1, 1991, seemed like any other fall day in Edmonds, Washington. That afternoon, glancing out my home office window, I noticed the misty rain typical for that time of year in the Northwest. Trees had already put on fall colors of yellow, orange, and brown. Oblivious to what the rest of the day would bring, I went back to work at my desk, looking over questionnaires handed in by those who had attended our seminars.

My husband, Dennis, was busy writing at the computer in his office, next to mine, on the other side of a book-lined wall. I thought of him as I contemplated our work together. His way with words, spoken or written, was one of his greatest gifts. There at the computer he most often felt God's presence. I looked at the computer sign he had made and hung on my office wall: "Christian writing is a conduit for God's thoughts to the world. It's a prophetic task, and it's important!" How true. Since resigning from his position as pastor of an active Episcopal church ten years earlier, he had had more time to pursue his writing projects.

I picked up my pencil, looked back at the pages on my desk, then looked past them thinking, *How I love his dimpled chin— the twinkle in his intelligent, deep blue eyes. He enjoys making people laugh with his spark of English humor. His jokes always make me laugh, too, even when I've heard them before; he tells them so well.*

Here I am, seventeen years his junior, and during his last two physically declining years, he's let me know that it's taking effort to keep up with my energy. I've willingly cut back on my Tuesday evening classes at church and tried to adjust in other ways. Dennis, though slight of build and average in height, is losing more weight than he should. That concerns me. Both of us were shocked at our twenty-fifth wedding anniversary, two weeks ago, when a physician friend proposed that Dennis's weight loss was his body compensating for his heart.

The cat scratching at my door brought me back from my reverie. Alex's greatest joy was getting into my office. He would jump up on my desk, walk over my computer keyboard, and plop himself down on a pile of letters or a manuscript. We made a game of seeing how long I could keep this seventeen-pound British shorthair out of my room. I had to keep my door closed or I'd never get anything done but scratching his ears.

I returned to the project at hand. At 5:45 the next scratch actually opened the door, which was not latched. As our same-color blue-green eyes met in this contest of wills, I laughed at him for his success at getting in.

"Oh, Alex," I said, chiding as he strutted victoriously into the room. It was a little past time for his supper, so I pushed back my chair and said, "Okay, you win. Let's get something to eat."

As we walked down the hall, I playfully batted at his long orange and white tail. As we passed Dennis's office, I looked in to say hello. I wasn't ready for what I saw.

One glance told me that my husband was dead. A moaned prayer escaped from me: "O God!" My first thoughts were deeply impressed on me, as though spoken: "He's gone." And then, "He made it!"

Dennis was still in his chair, which had fallen over backward on the floor. His blue face told the tale. The coloration resulted from the pooling of blood, his head lying lower than his legs.

I grabbed the phone and dialed 911. I told the operator the situation—Dennis was dead but still warm—and gave our address. As instructed and before hanging up the phone, I lifted him out of the chair and onto the floor. I did this from a kneeling position, wanting to be as tender and gentle as possible. But I quickly learned what "dead weight" means. I heard two cracking sounds in my back.

I moaned another prayer, "O Lord."

"I think I've injured my back," I told the woman on the phone, acknowledging some discomfort but no sharp pain. I gave CPR as guided, and within minutes the paramedics were at the door. They asked me to leave the room as they worked. Feeling as if I were in a dream, I phoned my family and my closest neighbor.

We knew Dennis had heart trouble. For years complications from his childhood rheumatic fever had been overcome. Then more recently, an Asian flu virus, picked up during travels, attacked his prolapsed heart valve, causing the return of a childhood heart murmur. With diminishing health, now at seventy-three years of age, he had made a decision: "Either God heals me or takes me home." With that statement he declined seeing a heart specialist, though he did see our family doctor. Months later, shortly after his seventy-fourth birthday—on All Saints' Day—God did "take him home." Dennis didn't want to die in a hospital, and he wanted a quick departure. Both wishes were granted.

My Healing

There at the house Dennis was pronounced dead. The medics carried me to the ambulance. Hospital X rays found two fractured vertebrae. This was all backward: I couldn't even honor my husband by accompanying his body to the funeral home.

I came home and laid on ice packs off and on for about two days. My physical healing progressed quickly. Before Dennis's funeral I was able to sit at my computer and plan his service, which I was able to attend. I walked down the aisle of St. Mark's Cathedral on the steady arm of Steve, Dennis's oldest son. The doctor had told me that with the help of physical therapy my back would be healed in twenty-one days. It was.

But it took a year and three-quarters, and much prayer, for my soul to be healed. My journey to wholeness took from November 1, 1991, to July 4, 1993. Many healing events occurred during that time.

The first few days, a family member or friend was at my house night and day to offer me comfort and support. Then two women alternated staying with me every night for the first month. (At first neither knew the other was doing this.) Another friend came for prayer when I called in emotional distress one evening. Many intercessors were praying.

I walked through the death scene and other related memories of that last day with my prayer partners a number of times before my emotions were healed. Through my experience and by praying with others, I've learned that the last day of the life of someone you love often warrants a great amount of prayer.

I journaled my feelings and responses from God to assist my healing. I had a number of comforting dreams about Dennis. I noted one on January 9, 1992: Dennis and I were walking together, and I asked him to tell me some of his jokes. We eventually stopped walking, and I said, "Thank God, you're here." He was smiling and looking great. "I want to kiss you," I said. And we had a wonderful long kiss.

Other people also had dreams of Dennis. One was very healing to me. On November 6, 1991, I received a letter (and later a visit) from the Rev. Don Goodheart, who said he was prompted by a dream to contact me and to talk to me about dreams. His visit and insights led me to look in my old files to find a dream that I had written down. I saw this dream, given on January 28, 1988, as being significant, in that it confirmed the timing of Dennis's death.

In my dream Dennis was very tired. He had been washing a beautiful plant. He showed me how the flower bud at the end of each branch could be taken off and put back on—like a light bulb that screws into a socket. There were three slightly opened blossoms and maybe four; I couldn't clearly see the fourth. Then I sat on his lap, laid my hand on his head, and prayed for him. After this dream I had written in my notes at the bottom of the page, "Perhaps this means Dennis has three more years and almost a complete fourth year." I shared this with no one; I filed it away, choosing to forget it.

But later when I realized that I'd had that dream three years and ten months before Dennis's death, I was elated with God's prophetic message to me. This was extremely helpful because of the suddenness of his death and lack of closure. I hadn't had a chance to say good-bye.

Then there was a climactic healing, like spiritual fireworks lighting the sky with blues and reds. It was even on the Fourth of July holiday, 1993. That afternoon my friend Shade O'Driscoll and I sat praying in my car, parked at Edmonds' beautiful waterfront. Through scriptural understanding and healing prayer, I received a panoramic view of our married life; the strands came together in such a way that it wove an amazing tapestry. I sensed a completion of my emotional healing, a reconciliation with my entire married life from beginning to end. This time of prayer, culminating others preceding it, brought total acceptance with every detail of our twenty-five years together, right down to the day of Dennis's death.

Set Your Mind on Heaven

In the healing of my soul (healing of memories and emotions), praying and being prayed for was vitally important. The second most helpful step was and is setting my mind on heaven.

The earthly picture of Dennis's death was quick but awful; death is never attractive. But the heavenly picture is that Dennis was ready to go. He had made his preparations for death by living his life fully committed to God. The kingdom of God was the center of his life.

We have to purposely set our minds on God, on things above and not on the earth. Every night I set my clock so that it will wake me at a certain hour. If I didn't set that clock, who knows when I would wake up? So it is with our minds. Scripture says to "set your mind on things above" (Col. 3:2 NKJV). The *Amplified* version says, "Set your minds and keep them set on what is above." Paul told the Ephesian Christians that they were (and we are) seated with Christ Jesus in heavenly places (Eph. 2:6). Believers' bodies are on earth, but our spirits are connected to heaven. The spirit, where God has been joined to us, has in a sense already ascended. The soul (or mind) is the area that has to be set on heavenly things. The earthly too often crowds out the heavenly.

I had been left with an all-too-vivid earthly picture of Dennis's passing. I needed to consider what things looked like from a heavenly vantage point. Here is what may have happened from heaven's perspective.

When Dennis's heart stopped, his spirit and soul separated from his body. Jesus says about a Christian's end, "I will come and get you" (John 14:3 TLB). The verse continues, "And if I go and prepare a place for you, I will come again and receive you to Myself; that where I am, there you may be also" (NKJV). This may be speaking especially of Christ's return at the end of the age, but I'd also like to consider it for us individually at the end of our age.

Met by Jesus, angels, and perhaps others, within a short time Dennis passed through the galaxies. (Dennis always enjoyed gazing at the planets and stars through his homemade telescope.) Arriving in heaven, he had a visual treat of colors in dimensions never seen before. A music lover, he may have heard singing beyond earth's greatest Caruso. He was met by and reunited to family, relatives, and friends. (These are guesses, of course.)

I cherish an even more vivid scene of how he may have entered heaven. The evening of Dennis's death, John Barrett, a former member of our church, had a dream. He described it to me:

"I saw a line of angels standing in a valley or pathway. The line was as long and far away as your eye can see. They were blowing trumpets. A Voice spoke as though it were introducing someone; I felt it was speaking to Dennis, though I couldn't see him. The

Voice said, 'Welcome home. Well done, my true and faithful servant.' Then the trumpets blew again. They were so loud that it woke me up!"

As I contemplated John's picture of heaven, I realized it was quite like what happens to royalty. When a king enters a ballroom or other public place, a trumpet sounds to proclaim his arrival. Then there is the announcement of who has arrived and the trumpet sounds again. I see Dennis being honored as royalty because he was and is a son of God who was faithful to the heavenly vision given him—faithful to the very end of his earthly days.

Which picture did you like best—the earthly or the heavenly one? I needed to process both pictures. The earthly one at first had loss, pain, disorientation, but eventually healing; both pictures are integrated together now. Through prayer the debris was cleared away so that my mind could be set on the perspective of eternal time.

As I set my mind on heaven, I found help through books I read and personal testimonies of those who had died and come back. They helped me release Dennis to the Lord's tender care.

An encouraging book that helped ease the pain of my loss was only sixty pages long, written by a woman who had experienced heaven during a four-day coma. Hers was not quite the same as a near-death experience, but it was close to it. Rebecca Springer's story, *Within the Gates*, was written nearly a hundred years ago and is still helping people today. I read a little bit from it each night; it was like taking a sedative. It was sent to me as a gift—the best gift I could have received, though I don't know who it came from. I wish Dennis and I could have read the book together before his departure. After reading that book, I savored every good book I could find on NDEs. A number written in the seventies were inspiring and sound.

When studying a topic, I want to hear from someone who has more information and more experience than I. Near-death accounts have many benefits. They tell how it feels to die; they are eyewitnesses to what people experience on the other side, and they give hope. It is encouraging to be reassured by a living, breathing human being that at death, for those who say yes to Christ, it is going to be okay—and truly more than okay. For the one in love with God—glorious.

The Bible has quite a bit to say about heaven, and a number of books have been written based on Scripture. Such resources are foundational. We will look specifically at the Bible's depiction of heaven in part 3 of this book.

Brief Descriptions of Stories Ahead

Would you like a taste of heaven? The heavenly viewpoint is what gives us hope and keeps us going. I have carefully chosen the following NDE stories. These NDEers are believers in God whose stories have a message of hope. Each testimony has encouraged me. None has been published in a book before, except one in a French edition of a book and one in a previous book of my own.

The first account is of Valvita Jones, now of Kansas, who at age twenty-seven had surgery with life-threatening complications. In her NDE she describes a loving encounter with Jesus, her own judgment by God the Father, and the joy of reconciliation. Deborah O'Donnell, a music teacher from Oregon, arrived at the city gate of heaven, where she found a message from God. Dr. Gerard Landry, a Texas medical doctor, died during a heart attack, entered heaven, and saw the eternal value of the Cross. Carolyn McCormick, a registered nurse from Oregon, had an encounter with angels that brought emotional healing to her. Pam Johnstone, a bank vice president from Washington state, got quite far into heaven, almost to the extent of crossing a bridge permanently.[1] Lorraine Tutmarc, a Seattle realtor before her retirement, was gloriously converted through her grueling but wonderful NDE. And Craig Gottschalk, then an eighteen-year-old from Seattle, appeared before the judgment throne of God; his story shows the power of a loved one's prayers.

A Time of Preparation

I am delighted to be able to share these messages with you. They, and others like them, have intensified what I already believed. They have lifted my soul from the not-so-lovely physical and earthly side of death and have helped prepare me for however my end may be.

In the last part of this book, I'll show you what the Bible says about heaven, a guided tour, so to speak. If you were going to take a trip to a foreign country, would you board the plane and then try to find out something about its weather, attractions, customs, dress, expenses, money exchange, and safety? No, I expect you would talk to a travel agent and study brochures to find the answers to your questions. Yet, many Christians have not studied about what heaven is like. They can tell you only a few details because they are so busy with this life that they don't have time to think about the next. I've been that way myself.

Some also have not prepared themselves for the journey. Before the flight, we need to have our shots, get our passports in order, have a trustworthy person take care of our belongings while we're gone, and say good-bye to those we're leaving behind. We need to be so ready that we have little else to do but get on the plane. In the pages that follow I will help you get ready for the trip of all time.

A nurse friend told me that she hadn't seen many patients who were happy at their end, even those who were professing Christians. This should not be, and I believe proper preparation can make a difference. For a believer in Christ, getting ready for death is getting ready for life at its fullest.

If my last journey is prolonged, not quick, I want someone to read this book to me (especially parts 2 and 3) to launch me into eternity. Also I'd like to hear the gospel of John in its entirety or at least chapter 1 (the greatness of God), chapter 10 (Jesus is the Good Shepherd; we're his sheep), chapter 17 (Jesus' last prayer for his people), chapter 19 (Jesus' death), and chapter 20 (Jesus' resurrection). If time allowed, I would also like to hear Psalm 23 (the Lord is my Shepherd), Psalm 139 (he is omnipresent), Isaiah 54 (a special chapter for widows and the childless), Acts 1 (Jesus' promised empowerment and his ascension), Acts 2 (God's Spirit poured out), Romans 8 (nothing can separate us from God's love), and Revelation 21–22 (the great pictures of heaven). I recently shared these Scripture references with a friend facing the death of a loved one. It helped her through her own distress and gave her guidance for what to read to her dying relative.

Some have found C. S. Lewis's children's book *The Last Battle* a help at the end. I myself would find that good reading because I love his books.

I urge you to set your mind on heaven and again to remember that heaven can heal your sorrow no matter what it may be. As you read, take time to look away from earth's troubles for a little while. Have a taste, a vision, a touch of the life to come. Let heaven bend down to embrace you, heal you, and give you hope.

Healing Prayer

Take a moment from the busyness of life to close your eyes and experience heaven enveloping you. Let God, who has compassion for you, give a heavenly perspective to your earthly sorrows. Let him heal, help, direct, change you. Take time here to talk to God about your needs. Listen for his voice, and then relax in his loving presence.

CHAPTER THREE

Crossing Through His Cross

Death is nothing else but going home to God; the bond of love will be unbroken for all eternity.

Mother Teresa
Blessed Are You

———◆———

I liked Valvita Jones right away when we met in 1992 at the KTBW TV studio, Federal Way, Washington. With a warm, ready smile, she was easy to talk to. That made our meeting enjoyable. Moreover, it was important because she was a guest I was interviewing on a program reaching a substantial audience across the Northwest.[1] This petite forty-three-year-old wore purple—a flowered skirt and top—and her dark brown hair was set off with a purple ribbon. Animated Valvita looked forward to her imminent flight east to her daughter's college graduation.

Valvita has a rich multiracial background, a combination of Cherokee, African American, and Caucasian. Her name comes from two Latin words: *val* meaning strong, and *vita* meaning life—a significant name to consider in light of her story.

At the time of her NDE, Valvita was a woman of faith, a wife, and the proud mother of a young daughter. She had recently lost a premature baby. Here she tells her story.

Setting the Stage

In 1974, three months after a cesarean section, I entered Kansas University Medical Center because I had a serious infection in my reproductive organs. Just before leaving for the hospital, I began thinking that I was going to die, though there wasn't any fear connected with it. As I looked at my relatives, a strange feeling came over me, as though I were seeing them for the last time.

While there, doctors tried antibiotics for several days to see if they could avoid major surgery, but they could not. I underwent a hysterectomy and all seemed well. Recuperating in the hospital three days later, I began feeling strange. Something was very wrong, so I called a nurse. Doctors discovered that I had double pneumonia, a blood clot, internal bleeding, and kidney failure.

Fighting for Life

Doctors rushed me to X ray, and during the tests I drifted in and out of consciousness. At one point I heard the doctor in a loud voice asking the nurse to check my blood pressure. I heard the nurse answer, "Zero. Zilch." I realized they were fighting for my life.

Through all this physical trauma, I was talking to God and saying, "Why me? Why now?" I didn't want to die. I was asking God, "Why?" I never thought I'd say that, but I found myself questioning my situation, especially since something wonderful had happened while I was in the hospital. You see, we were about to adopt a son who had *just* been born. He and I were lying in the very same hospital.

My inner fight to live was taking every ounce of energy. I was trying to hold on to life for the people I loved—my daughter and my husband, Walter. Pictures reeled through my mind of him coming to the hospital and finding me gone. I was praying a lot, asking for God's help.

Finally I realized what I was doing—trying to maintain control of my life. But if I was God's child and if it was my time to go, I should surrender myself. I asked him to forgive me for complaining, and I was at peace.

I then became extremely conscious of my breathing. It became slower and slower—a longer time between each breath. And each breath became deeper and deeper. I had never breathed so deeply in all my life. I started counting "one, two," and the third breath was the deepest, as if it came from my feet up. Then it was as if I became that third breath. Though I was that breath, I still knew I was a whole person.

Met by Jesus

Feeling so peaceful and free, I started moving upward. I realized my body was below me, and I vaguely remember observing efforts by the medical team to revive it. My main interest was that I was above the room. I was not even in the room but in the first sky. I say first sky in the heavens, because it seemed as though there were three heavens that I passed through.

At the first heaven I met a Being. Or I should say he met me. I recognized him as Jesus Christ, and he led me through the three heavens. When I think about Jesus' physical presence, it almost fades away, because the predominant feature is that he is love through and through. As I recall, he had dark brown wavy hair and an olive complexion. I looked into his eyes. They were piercing but loving and as clear as blue water. You could almost see yourself mirrored in his eyes. When he looked at you, he looked straight through you and into you. You realized immediately that he knew all there was to know about you.

There now seemed to be a heavenly illumination that caused his hair to be light red and his eyes bluish, almost transparent, and his skin a light golden color. There is no way to fully describe his coloring. It is like another world's color. It's the Shekinah glory, iridescent golden light glowing through him. In his resurrection body, his coloring is uniquely different from anything on earth.

Before the Most High

I'll tell you what happened in the three heavens. The first heaven was light blue in color but brilliant and so unlike anything I've seen that I can't fully describe it. It opened up, split down the middle as though along a seam, and both sides rolled back like paper scrolls. This happened as fast as a snap of my fingers. We went through two more skylike heavens, which also rolled back one after the other.

In a matter of seconds I found myself before the Most High. *The Most High* is the term I use because I recognized the presence of God the Father. In looking at him, I couldn't really see him, but there was an awesome glory, an awesome presence. You could feel it everywhere, and I realized that he was on the throne. When I tried to see what the throne was like, I discovered it was invisible. I knew it was there; I just could not *see* it. It was so big that it extended all the way to earth; earth is part of that throne. This was an incredible awareness. Stunned by it all, I felt as small as a little ant, so insignificant. Trembling, I found myself prostrate. While I was lying there on my face, he spoke to me. It was unlike the mental speech between Christ and me, because the Father sounded like many waters rushing. I lay there a very long time, with God speaking to my soul. The words he spoke to me can't be recalled, but they were about me and my life.

As I lay there I relived every instance of my existence, every emotion and thought. I saw why I was the way I was; I reexperienced the way I had dealt with people and they with me. I saw where I could have done better. I felt emotions I was ashamed of, yet I realized there were things I had done well and felt good about. As we looked at different scenes, I would respond, "Yes, I see how I could have done it another way, a better way." I wondered how anyone could feel worthy in God's presence. I wasn't condemned, but I didn't feel worthy. It's hard to explain. The whole time that was going on, for how long I don't know, I kept praising God.

With the ending of my life review, I felt absolutely unworthy of being there in the presence of this magnificent Light, unworthy in comparison to the grand scheme of things. *It is all so beautiful, and what am I?* I said this to God. Then Jesus' hand touched me, and I was able to get back on my feet because I had previously had no strength. Taking me by the hand, he led me to the side of a main arena. He looked into my eyes, into my soul, and I knew he knew and understood everything I felt. When he looked into me, it was with more love than I ever thought possible for anyone to know. He smiled, one look letting me know everything would be all right.

The Bridge

With this reassuring look he led me to one side. He stepped away from me and went alone into the light. Where Christ's light ended and God the Father's began, I cannot say. They both gave off light and their light was the same light. I will never forget this as long as I live. When Christ had stepped away from me, he turned sideways and stretched out his arms as a bridge. One arm extended to me and one to the Father. His arms were extended as if they were making a cross and a bridge to cross over.

It was like a visual representation of the Scripture: "For there is one God and one mediator between God and men, the man Christ Jesus, who gave himself as a ransom for all" (1 Tim. 2:5–6). God is on one side, and all people are on the other side. Jesus himself is between human beings and his Father to bring them to him. Christ made this possible by giving his life for all people. Everything I knew from Scripture was flashing into my mind.

Then I heard the Father and Son communing about my case. Jesus said, "My blood is sufficient. She's mine." When he said that, all the doubts about my unworthiness disappeared. I jumped up and down, shouting and rejoicing. I have never been so happy in all my life! The kind of love I felt is beyond explanation. I kept saying, "Oh, my God. Oh, my God. This is my Mediator. This is my Advocate." Just as I read in the Bible.

Jesus came back to where I was and looked at me again with comforting love. We rejoiced together. He went on teaching me and talking to me a lot, but I don't recall the details. Now being so free and so loved, I never wanted to leave his side. I told him so, but a look in his eyes said I had to return.

I asked, "Must I really leave?"

He looked at me with tenderness and said, "Yes, because there is a work I have for you to do."

Coming back into my body in intensive care was as quick as my journey out had been. It seemed like the speed of light. Christ brought me back. I looked at his sweet face for the last time, a face I could have looked at forever. Next thing I knew, I was looking into the face of a friend who had gotten into intensive care by saying she was my sister. I didn't realize where I was. When I saw her face, I was shocked because Jesus was gone so fast.

Looking for his face but seeing her face, I was disappointed. She told me later there was a look on my face that she had never seen before. She was confused—and a little hurt—by my response to her. After a full explanation later, she realized that I truly had been happy to see her.

Changed Life

Following my recovery, I took an art class in oil painting. I kept trying to capture the "colors of Jesus" on canvas. That's all I could paint. I painted him in all colors, all styles, but it is impossible to capture that color. The students lovingly teased me, saying I was a "Jesus girl."

But my obsession with painting Jesus was a mild change compared to other areas of my life. Perhaps the biggest turnabout was my point of view. Before my NDE I used to fuss and bicker with Walter about petty concerns. I had wanted many things for myself. When I came back, I had a different appreciation for human relationships. They are so important. Much of what we think of as important isn't important at all.

In 1986 I felt the Lord telling me, "Feed my sheep." This was at a time when Walter and I had begun a shelter for the homeless. We were called to that work for several years. I guess there are different ways we can feed his sheep or his lambs. Care of children is another way, and currently I'm a foster parent. We care for five children in our home.

After having this fantastic near-death experience, I thought I should be doing big, wonderful projects for God. He has shown me that life is not about doing big things, but about doing whatever I do for him. While I was in heaven, God did not give me a specific commission that I know of, but my strongest sense is that my purpose is to love.

Reflection

A poem written by Valvita in 1994 shows how she gained a strong sense of her identity as a woman and as a child of God.

I am black
I am red
I am white
the daughter of a legacy of wealth
I am the descendant of slaves

> *the reminder of a lost dynasty*
> *I am the lineage of the first people*
> *the overture of pain from a stolen land*
> *I am the flame of passion*
> *the daughter of love*
> *I am the blood of all my ancestors*
> *the seed of hope eternally continuing*
> *I am the mother of faith*
> *the sister of peace*
> *I am the friend of joy*
> *the acquaintance of sorrow*
> *I am the voice crying out for equality*
> *the torch of liberty*
> *I am as hands of God*
> *as feet of Christ*
> *I am a creation of God*
> *the rib of man*
> *I am the clay that became a living soul*
> *I am woman.*

Love . . . Can there be a higher calling? Bernard of Clairvaux put it this way: "Life is only for love. Time is only that we might find God."[2]

What an awesome picture it was to see Jesus standing as a bridge between Valvita and God the Father to reconcile her to her Father in heaven. Each of us comes to the Father through Jesus' purity, not our own.

Healing Prayer

Jesus' loving arms are stretched out to you. He wants to be your Mediator, your Advocate. Can you see yourself with a load of guilt, pain, and sin slung over your shoulder in a sack? Will you walk out to meet Jesus and give him your load? Ask his forgiveness? Even now he is there to meet you and take that burden to the Father to plead your case in the courts of heaven. You can know the joy that Valvita experienced when you hear him say to you, "You're free. You're forgiven. Come, follow me." Take time to feel the joy, the lightness that forgiveness brings. Wait and experience.

CHAPTER FOUR

I Was in Heaven While My Baby Slept in Her Crib

Fear not, for I have redeemed you;
I have called you by your name;
You are Mine.
When you pass through the waters, I will be with you.

God the Father
Isaiah 43:1–2 NKJV

———◆———

Music is Deborah O'Donnell's life. In high school she played the reed organ in an Episcopal mission in Auburn, Nebraska. There she became a Christian in 1946. In 1969 Deborah earned her B.A. in music, and since then she has taught voice and piano to children who come to her home studio. Deborah has also raised four children and loves being a homemaker.

When close mutual friends, Dr. and Mrs. Keith Oles, told me their longtime friend Deborah had an inspiring story to tell, I arranged to meet her. In the fall of 1993 I interviewed her during a conference I was attending in Eugene, Oregon. There, this rather angelic-looking musician, with shoulder-length auburn hair and deep blue eyes, told me her story:

Setting the Stage

What I'm about to tell you happened twelve years before Ted, my first husband, died in 1976—hence, in June l964, four months after the birth of my daughter, my fourth child. I had many problems after her delivery, including hemorrhaging, so I stayed very quiet for several months. Then we went to our cabin on the McKenzie River.

At the cabin we had pine needles to sweep off the roof, so while the baby slept in her crib and the older children played in the woods, Ted and I went to work. Ted would not let me get up on the roof. I stood on the ladder and did what I could from there, sweeping what I could reach. He was sweeping from the top of the roof. The two of us together were making quite a cloud of dust, and dirt was flying into my face. I could feel it collecting in my throat. When we took our break, I said, "I have to go in and gargle some of this dirt out of my throat."

Ted rested in one of the lawn chairs in the front yard while I went into the house. I remember walking into the bathroom and standing at the sink to gargle the debris out of my throat. I must have inhaled dirt into my windpipe, for I fell to the floor unconscious.

The Journey

Next thing I knew, I was lying in a bed in a room I didn't recognize. The atmosphere was so beautiful, beyond anything I could naturally imagine. I could feel love and joy and peace in the air. I thought, *I must be dead. I must have died.* But when I pinched myself, I felt it, and that confused me.

I got out of bed and walked out of the building. There were people around, but they didn't speak to me. I don't remember all the details of the setting, but I do recall the incredible beauty of everything. People seemed very happy and calm. There was a gardener working with the plants. The grass was greener and the sky bluer than I'd ever seen! I thought, *I must be in heaven!*

I started toward the main street, outside the building. The street—a beautiful highway—looked like golden bricks. *If this is heaven,* I thought, *soon I'm going to see my mother and my father, or my grandmother and my grandfather.* I was so excited about that! I'd lost a lot of important people.

Then I thought, *No—the greatest thing of all is that I'm going to see Jesus!* Joy welled up from way down inside me. I

started to run, thinking, *I can hardly wait to see him!* I had no
memory of whom I had "left behind"—my husband or children—
only of those who were there in heaven!

When I started to run down the street of gold, I was pulled
back, pulled away, even though I was fighting with all my might to
stay, because I didn't want to leave the path.

As I was pulled out and up into the air, I saw that heaven was
like a city. I could see a wall around it, and I could look into it, as
if I were viewing it from an airplane. There was a massive gate at
the entrance of this city. I wondered if this were the gate to the city
of Jerusalem. Over this gate I saw words written in huge golden
letters. (This was interesting, especially because no one had yet
said anything to me.) The words arched over the gate said, "You
will return, but I have work for you to do."

The Return and Reentry

With that I "came back." Immediately I thought I had died. I
was unable to move at first. My eyes were wide open when I came
to. My feet were in the bathroom in front of the sink and stool. The
door being left open, I had fallen with the rest of my body landing
in the tiny hallway. My head was in the corner of the hall, which
was, in some way, the backdrop for a review of every phase of my
life. As life came back to me, my earthly memory bank returned. I
had been a premature baby who wasn't supposed to live. Being so
long in the incubator, the nurses had called me Inky, my mother
had told me.

I now relived that experience—not as one observing from the
outside. Staring into that corner of the hall, I was an infant in the
incubator where I had lain three months. I could see the glass walls
of the incubator around me. It was easy to breathe because of the
steady flow of oxygen. It seemed a warm and comforting place.

Then I was in my crib playing with my toys. Next I was three
years old, when I nearly died from whooping cough. After that I
was in first grade enjoying school. Then I was ten years old, when
my dear grandmother died. Sick with bronchitis, I was unable to
attend her funeral. I cried for three days. I remembered a dream
that calmed my spirit. My grandmother was in the dream; I was

told "Dee [my nickname], it is all right." I sat straight up and saw
a tall man in iridescent light at the foot of my bed. Guessing him to
be an angel, I said "Michael? Gabriel?" *Oh, it couldn't be Jesus.*
"Jesus?" With that a wonderful peace enveloped me, and I slept
soundly.

On through life I went; I was married and had four children.
My memories, mixed with the awareness of God's omnipresence,
gave me peace. I thought, *I'm back.*

Getting up, I shook myself. There was something in my
throat. I spit it into the sink; it was a mixture of red and black.
Blood mixed with dirt, I thought. I filled a glass with water and
took a drink to see if everything was working all right. I had no
problem swallowing, and the water refreshed me.

I came out of the bathroom feeling a little disoriented. Was
it a dream? Was I losing my mind? No, I couldn't have dreamed that
incredibly beautiful place. The air had been like breathing in love,
peace, and joy. My mind was tracking well, and I had physically
choked, so it wasn't merely my imagination. I would have to think
this experience over for a while.

As I walked back to join Ted in the yard, I mused, *No one will
believe this, especially Ted. He's been fighting my spiritual quest,
so I can't tell him what just happened.* At the time he almost
seemed jealous of my relationship with God. I could just imagine
how he would respond. The doctor's office was quite a distance
from our cabin, and going there would mean I'd have to explain
things to Ted. So I didn't tell him—or see a doctor.

I walked out into the yard and sat down on the lawn chair
next to Ted. "Do you know how long I've been gone?"

"I'd say about fifteen, or more like twenty, minutes."

We rested for a while. I thought, *There I was in heaven,
while my baby Jeanette was asleep in her crib.* Ted interrupted
my reverie. "Do you want to go up on the roof and help me finish
the job?"

"Let me go in and check on Jeannette," I answered, "and then
I'll be back to help you. But I have a request to make."

"What's that, dear?"

"Please be careful not to sweep debris in my direction."

Off and on for quite a few days confusion about my experience dogged me. I carefully evaluated the scene, going over it again and again. Finally I was convinced that it was real. Though I was sure no one would believe me, I knew it had happened. I now had a wonderful secret that I could tell no one. I knew I had died, gone to heaven, and come back.

Afterward

I realized I had been "sent back" to earth because I still had work to complete. In part, that was, of course, raising my children. But God also wanted to use me to draw Ted closer to him. Ted had been fighting the Holy Spirit for many years.

The Lord kept saying in my heart, "I'll work through you to reach him."

I kept saying, "Lord, please send someone else!"

That November, the same year as my NDE, I came into a deep sense of being filled with the Holy Spirit. Nine months later I felt strong enough to risk telling Ted about my near-death experience. True to form, Ted got extremely angry. He always seemed unhappy when I received strength from God rather than from him. For several years he rejected my experience, not wanting to believe it.

Meanwhile my enthusiasm for God continued to increase. My friends and I pooled our resources and started a tape and book ministry. Each week we would listen to a new cassette of a Spirit-filled speaker and pray for one another. Many wives took a tape home to share with their husbands. Ted tolerated these meetings because they took place while he was at work.

My compassion for others also increased. I wanted to share more with people who were sick or spiritually hungry. When visiting the sick, I would ask if they wanted me to pray for them. I became an evangelist to many.

One day, to my utter amazement, Ted asked me to pray for him to receive Jesus and an infilling of the Holy Spirit. Following this, it seemed he fell in love with God. He repeatedly thanked me for my patience and perseverance with him. Our love grew as a result of God's love drawing us together.

Another result of my NDE is that I have absolutely no fear of death now! I even silently prayed, "Dear God, please don't take my husband before you take me back." But that was not his will. When Ted died in 1976, I was not fearful for him. There was a complete peace about the whole thing, although his death was quite sudden and unexpected. I now have been happily married for fourteen years to Robert, and we have five grandchildren.

As I said before, I have no fear of dying. I'm eager to go back whenever the time is right. I am ready. I feel very secure and know that no matter what I must go through, I rest in the palm of God's hand.

Reflection

Here a whole family was oblivious to the fact that they almost lost their mother. A husband sat in the yard not knowing that his wife was having a glimpse of the eternal city. She went to the bathroom to gargle the accumulation of debris from her throat and twenty minutes later came out a new person. Perhaps this wonderful testimony can help us remember that miracles are happening all around us, but unless we have eyes to see them, we will miss them.

I see strong evidence that Deborah died and returned, in that following her experience she had no fear of death. All humans have a basic fear of death; people don't suddenly get over this kind of fear for no reason at all. Dr. Michael Sabom, whom I quoted in chapter 1, surveyed 106 people who had been near death about their fear of death. Of forty-five people who had not had an accompanying NDE, thirty-nine claimed no change in their fear; one had increased fear, and one had decreased fear. Of sixty-one patients who had had an NDE, eleven claimed no change in their fear, while fifty had a decrease in fear of death.[1]

Deborah already knew the One who conquered death, and this relationship was the foundation for release of fear as she was near death. Others who felt a release, as shown in the above survey, most likely had a heavenly encounter on their journey. The memorable Scripture passage asks a rhetorical question: "O death, where is thy sting?" (1 Cor. 15:55 KJV). The next verse answers,

"The sting of death is sin." The Bible goes on to say that death and its sting were dealt with at the Cross. Here is found the only true antidote—one that is effective for all who believe in God's Son, the One who died and came back, never to die again. He brought not only victory over the human condition of sin, but victory over the fear of death as well.

Deborah's release from this basic fear was more powerful for her having read God's personal message to her arched over the gate of heaven. What a confidence builder to receive from God, Creator of the universe, the message "You will return, but I have work for you to do."

Teaching piano and voice to children is a special calling that doesn't go unnoticed by God. What an enriching gift music is to a child. While recovering from a mild stroke this year, Deborah was encouraged by the mother of one of her students, who said, "A lot more children need you." That helped Deborah get back to her studio; she's teaching again and loving it.

Healing Prayer

You, too, have been chosen for a special work on this planet. Do you know what it is? You may ask, *What would God want with me?* The answer is "Plenty." You are needed. If you aren't on talking terms with God, it is going to be hard to get his message. In addition to that, he has left a whole book of messages with you in mind. Take time to read his Book, the Bible, daily.

Now close your eyes and picture the gate of heaven—God's front door. Ask Jesus to give you a message, a calling. Wait in his presence.

CHAPTER FIVE

A Doctor's Story

Day by day we are building for eternity. . . . Every gentle word, every generous thought, every unselfish deed will become a pillar of eternal beauty in the life to come.

Rebecca Springer
Within the Gates

Love never fails.

1 Corinthians 13:8 NKJV

———◆———

A message sent at an opportune moment can bring great comfort and encouragement. In the fall of 1991 my oldest brother, Bill (Dr. William S. Reed), sent me such a message. It was a cassette tape on which one of his colleagues told the story of his own death and return experience. The talk had been given for doctors attending a conference in Tampa, Florida.[1] Bill sent this message to give me encouragement during the early days of my grief. I played it over many times and was greatly helped. I also made numerous copies for others.

Dr. Gerard Landry and I had agreed to meet in early December of 1996 at the Dallas/Fort Worth Airport for our first face-to-face visit. I was returning home after teaching my weekend course on the Lord's Prayer, and he was seeing his wife off. He was waiting at my departure gate as I approached, and I immediately knew who he was. Dr. Landry was nicely dressed in casual attire and of average height and weight. *His curly white hair, warm eyes, and gentle smile would give a patient total confidence,* I thought. We shook hands and sat down.

"Dr. Landry, I'm so glad to finally meet you," I said. "Now I've met every one of the seven people in my book who've been to heaven." He grinned and said that he was happy to meet me too. We had a wonderful visit, spoke of heaven (of course!), and ended by praying for one another. What a great sendoff after a delightful weekend.

Gerard Landry has had an interesting medical career. Graduating from Laval Medical College in Quebec in 1951 and doing postgraduate studies at the University of Nebraska Medical College, he served in various branches of medicine—anesthesiology, industrial medicine, family practice, and emergency medicine. Now semiretired, Gerard is director of anesthesia at an eye clinic in Tyler, Texas.

He is a positive and ambitious person. He and his wife, Denise, have eight children ranging in age from twenty-six to forty-four.

I trust Dr. Landry's story will help you as it did me. Walk with him now through a miracle that defies a medical explanation.

Setting the Stage

What I have to share is a tremendous miracle in my life, and it may help you at some time in your future. It is an experience where my heart stopped for approximately four minutes. I'm fortunate to be alive to tell you what I went through.[2]

I had worked twenty-seven years in medicine, and Denise and I had a very good life. In 1978 I decided to take a sabbatical, so in September my wife, three of our children, and I left for Israel for nearly six months.

We returned home to Texas in March. Two weeks later, on a cool Saturday morning—March 24, 1979—Denise and I spent an hour reminiscing about our inspiring journey to such a historic land, thanking God for our opportunity. We also prayed for our children and friends. After our time together and a good lunch, I went outside and brought in two armfuls of wood for the fireplace. As I walked in the door, a tiredness suddenly came over me as I had never felt before. In fact, I had never been sick in my life. The sense of fatigue was overwhelming. Setting the wood down by the fireplace, I told my wife that I didn't feel well.

"Well, dear, why don't you rest?" she suggested.

I sat down, trying to relax, when a severe pain started in the middle of my chest. I will describe it as a physician can best describe his own MI (myocardial infarction). It was like a Mack truck barreling over my chest. Or at least like the largest man in the room, wearing a size fourteen shoe, standing on my chest and staying there. It was a severe, crushing pain.

"This is serious, Denise!" With great urgency I cried out, "Let's pray!"

I asked God that his mercy and love would be poured upon Denise and me. And then and there it was as if a shower of love poured down. An indescribable peace settled on both of us. I had never before felt such depth of peace. We were then able to call an ambulance. The peace that came over me is hard to describe to others because it is a living experience. One has to go through it to understand.

Now mind you, I still had the pain. I was sure this was an MI—a massive heart attack. The pain was still there, but it was bearable.

The ambulance took us to the hospital emergency room, arriving at 4:00 P.M. A very young doctor, an intern, met us. I described the pain and told him I was having an MI. He didn't waste any time.

I had worked in that same emergency room for many years, so I knew exactly what was going on. This knowledge probably allayed some fear, because I had done to other patients the same things they were doing to me. Right away a lifeline—intravenous solution—was started, and I was given an electrocardiogram.

The doctor showed me the test results and said, "You've had a massive MI." My wife was standing by my bed in the emergency room. Hearing this diagnosis, she put her hand on my chest and forehead and prayed. I immediately felt the presence of God.

Awareness of Eternity

Suddenly, in a flash, I couldn't think. At 4:13 P.M. I was transported from the physical realm, the realm of the body, to a spiritual realm. I knew I was in another world—a world that is as real as this world is to anyone reading this. What I saw I saw with the eyes of the spirit, because at that time my soul and my spirit were in heaven. At the time you leave the flesh, your spiritual awareness becomes acute, because the flesh holds down your spiritual awareness. At death your spirit is released. My experience was supernatural but nonetheless real.

The first awareness was of eternity. How can I describe eternity to you? I'll give you an example. Our time dimension was created by God when he created the world. We need time to help us function properly. We need sleep to help rejuvenate our bodies.

For thousands of years, time was measured by sunrise and sunset. Humankind then developed various ways to tell time from the study of the heavens, to sundials, and clocks. Then came the wrist-watch, which has become increasingly sophisticated. Now we have digital watches.

At one time, the measurement of time in seconds was unknown to us. Now seconds are broken into fractions, even to one billionth of a second called a nanosecond. That is faster than you can blink an eye. What we did not know in the past has now become known to us through inventions coming from study in the fields of physics and mathematics. Calculations of computer scientists are amazing.

Such inventions can also bring us to a greater understanding of eternity. For instance, we measure time by hours, minutes, seconds, microseconds, and nanoseconds. When we die everything stops. It is like finally getting to the nanosecond, where time stops for us. Like a watch, our body stops at that time. Yet our spirit and consciousness continue to live on in a dimension beyond sequential time. We go beyond nanoseconds into a space-time measurement we cannot know here on earth. I call it the eternal *now*, because that is how it felt to me. The past, present, and future are all merged into what Scripture calls eternity. Eternity is the present, the now that never ends.

Truly understanding this dimension requires a joining of the human spirit to the Holy Spirit. As this connection happens, we go beyond head knowledge to heart experience. Jesus came expressly to give us this kind of life—eternal life. He told us about it. He demonstrated it. He imparted it.

Then, as if I had eyes all around my head, I saw saints, souls that were in heaven—multitudes. There was no way to count them. Whether there were millions or billions, I have no idea. As far as I could see in every direction were people of all sizes dressed in white robes. The people were transparent; I could see through them. They were behind me, across from me, all around me. They were "floating" on what appeared to be a crystal mirror or cloud or smoke. It is hard to describe these things in earthly terms, but I am trying to show you what my spirit saw. Each person was holding a crown in his or her hand. The saints were saying, "We were waiting for you."

I looked at my body and realized I was one of them. When you look at yourself and can look through yourself, it is quite an experience. I was looking at a form of my body.

Love Revealed

Then the clouds seemed to be separating (yet they were not actually clouds), and Jesus appeared. When he appeared, he showed himself to me on the cross as if he were in the flesh, still with his nail-pierced hands and feet, the wound in his side. To me this signified that the cross will be remembered forever in heaven and that the salvation it brings is forever.

If I tried to describe what he looked like, the color of his eyes and all, my words would be inadequate. It would be like seeing a picture and then trying to describe what it was like to experience the person.

Then Jesus glanced at me with a look of compassion, full of love and caring. A glance similar, I imagine, to the look he gave his mother, Mary, and his friend John as they waited in agony at the foot of the cross. This glance was the essence of love. *I understood the fullness of the love of God at that moment*. This glance must have been like the one Jesus gave Matthew at the tax collector's table. Jesus probably just stopped, looked at him, and said, "Follow me."

I also saw the perfect obedience that Jesus has for his Father. He obeyed him on the cross. He died on the cross for us because he loves his Father and he loves us. In love he became a servant for us. All the things I had read in the Bible became real to me right then.

Jesus spoke with a voice that relayed the same love his glance transmitted to me—such gentleness and tenderness. Once you hear it, you will never forget it.

He welcomed me with, "Gerry, my peace be with you"—my first name, then peace be with you. He said, "You are healed. You will feel no pain. You will have no anxiety. You will have no fears or guilt from the past. In one week you will be home from the hospital." When Jesus said, "You are healed," I thought, *Lord, it is wonderful in this place. I want to stay.*

He also told me that all the prayers we had prayed that morning would be answered or were right then being answered. And he said, "Go and tell your family, your friends, your fellowship, and everyone you come in contact with; tell them about my love. I want you to read the gospel of John, the first two letters of John, and all of Revelation."

"Lord," I said, "why do you want me to do this?"

He said, "John is my friend. He knows all about my love."

I didn't fully realize what was happening—that my heart had stopped for four minutes and that I was being brought back to life. When the Lord finished talking to me, I was aware that I was back in my body. I then entered a deep coma in which I was unable to communicate or move any part of my body for more than ten hours.

Hospital Happenings

When I came out of the coma, I became aware of my surroundings. It was three o'clock in the morning. I was in the intensive care unit. When I saw all the paraphernalia around, I said, "What is this, anyway?" I didn't know I had gone through a cardiac arrest.

I cried out, "I want to go back to be with Jesus." The young nurse on duty tried to comfort me. I went to sleep off and on, reliving my wonderful experience with my Lord.

This is what my physician later told me. They fought for my life in the emergency room when my heart was stopped for four minutes. A life-or-death "code 44" went through the whole hospital. They administered external cardiac massage, and I had two shock treatments. Once they got "regular" heartbeats, they were quite arrhythmic for a while. I vomited the meal I had taken at noon. I aspirated, and the vomit entered into one of the bronchial tubes, causing my right lung to collapse. They suctioned and suctioned. I went into convulsions, and I was on a respirator for a number of hours, unable to breathe on my own.

Healing Beyond the Natural

In Israel, playing volleyball just before we returned home, I had broken my little finger. Three weeks later, at the time of my heart attack, it was still very swollen and painful to touch, and I couldn't bend it at all. But after I came out of the coma, later that Sunday I looked at my little finger. I said with amazement, "It is healed. I can bend my finger. It is completely normal, with no pain."

I looked at my chest. Usually there would be a burn where they had put the electrodes on my chest for the shock treatment, but there was nothing there, no marks. Neither was there pain where the resuscitation team had pushed hard on my chest for four minutes.

That Sunday afternoon, sitting in my bed, I read half the gospel of John. I wanted to read what Jesus had told me to read: the gospel of John, John's first two epistles, and John's Revelation. I wanted to dig in there as soon as possible.

The doctor came in and said, "The results of your CPK [creatine phosphokinase] and all the enzymes are extremely high. It will be a long time for your recovery." That was not a happy report. The next day, however, he said, "I cannot understand it. Your heart enzymes and CPK came down from a high 3,800 to 400." Then the following day it was normal.

One week later I was up and about. Monday, a week later, the doctor did many EKGs and had the whole battery of tests repeated to see if there was any heart damage.

He said, "Well, you know, you have a little scar there, but everything is within normal limits. All I can do is send you home. I don't see any reason why you should be kept here."

From the time I came out of my coma I have had no angina or pain in my muscles—nothing. The X ray they took Monday morning was back to normal. The atelectatic (collapsed) lung condition I had in the ER was gone. So I, a medical doctor, say that Jesus Christ must receive the glory for this wonderful healing miracle.

When I was still in the coma, Denise called people in the church, asking them to pray for me. As I said, Jesus had told me my prayers would be answered. I didn't realize that this included my healing, salvation of all our family, our household, and all the things that we had prayed for that very morning.

Memories of a Watching Wife

While Dr. Landry was experiencing a taste of heaven, Denise was by his side urgently praying that God would spare his life. Here she shares some of her recollections and reflections of the trauma:

I was grateful that I had already learned how to pray and didn't wait for that desperate moment to learn how. As I stood there in the emergency room, thoughts crowded my mind. If this was Gerry's call to leave, I knew he was ready, but was I ready to let him go? If I were left alone, I'd need to finish raising the children by myself. Losing Gerry would leave such a hole in our family—and in me.

Then later in the waiting room I opened the Bible. In Psalm 80 I read that God rescued his people Israel from their calamities. I put Gerry's name wherever I read *Israel* and asked the Lord for Gerry's life. I prayed earnestly to God. We also had many other people praying for him.

In intensive care I had no idea what had happened to Gerry except that the physician told me he had gone through a severe heart attack. Further instructions later were that he would have to stay quiet for probably a month in the hospital and another month at home. (I was just grateful to have him back.) That isn't what happened. As Jesus had told him, Gerry was totally healed, and he was home in one week!

I thanked God then, and, of course, now, for doctors and hospitals. Sometimes doctors' families kind of resent hospitals and the profession because the work of a physician so often takes him or her away from family and home. I was thankful also for all the technology we benefit from and how this, coupled with prayer, provided a way to overcome my husband's illness.

In the intensive care unit Gerry was awake, lying on a narrow bed, tubes still attached to him. I touched him, and he said, "Oh, Denise, I saw Jesus, and he looks just like you and me."

Joyfully surprised, I said, "Oh, isn't that incredible!" I'd read some experiences of people going to heaven and coming back, but now Gerry, my own dear husband, had actually experienced this. It was marvelous.

Gerry said, "Do you know what Jesus told me? He told me that your prayer was answered when you 'prayed in the Spirit.' He also told me it was answered because you are such a wonderful woman."

Now that really shocked me, and I had to step back because I know I am not a "wonderful woman." Like anyone else, I fail and am far from being perfect. When I do fail, I confess my sins, which brings me into right standing with God and with others.[3] Yet I couldn't believe Jesus would say that about me. As I thought about it, I realized he loves all of us that way; his children are all wonderful. God loves us far more than we love ourselves.

I stood there looking at Gerry, and he began to weep, tears flowing down his face. Can you imagine what it looked like, with the tubes in his nose, the IV hooked up, and him weeping? He said, "Jesus told me that he loves, he loves, he loves." He kept repeating, "Jesus loves, and he loves, and he loves." He couldn't stop these words as the tears trickled down his cheeks. Gerry still weeps when he tells his story, because experiencing the depths of Jesus' love is overwhelming.

The next morning—Sunday—I went to church. One of the men told me about what had happened while he had been praying for Gerry at 3:00 A.M.—precisely when Gerry came out of the coma. Right then he felt sure that Gerry would live and that he would bring the message of Jesus' love to many people, especially those in his profession. That is what has happened ever since.

Commissioned to Tell

Gerry finishes his own story.

Jesus commissioned me to tell everyone about his love. I have made no effort to seek people to tell my experience to. Yet almost every day God has given me someone with whom to share my experience and his message. Even late at night he has sometimes sent people to our home. I talk to patients. Hundreds of cassette tapes have gone to many hospitals and to relatives and friends. I have never pushed it. They ask for it. I know this is God's doing.

All I want to tell people is about the love of Jesus, that eternal love he showed me. I have pondered why this happened to me. As I look back I realize Jesus baptized me with his love. That is all I can tell you. I think he looked at my heart, which had an area that was somewhat hardened, and said, "I'm going to take a branding iron and brand on your heart a mark, a scar that will be left there. It will be love, my love, and it will be branded on your heart for the rest of your days."

Dying, for someone who loves the Lord, is not a pain. There is no agony. That is the greatest thing I seek now. I look forward to the day that I'll go back and be with the Lord. When you live a life committed to him, you have said, "Lord, I love you. I belong to you. You are in me. You are in my heart." The people who do this have already made a testimony—with their lips and their lives. In heaven we will be received just like the other souls who are already there.

I'd like to share Romans 8:35–39 with you:

> Who can separate us from the love of Christ? Can trouble do it? Or hardship? Or persecution? Or hunger? Or poverty? Or danger? *Or death*? As the Scripture says, for your sake we are in danger of death at all times. We are treated like sheep that are going to be slaughtered. No, in all things we have complete victory through him who loves us. For I am certain that nothing can separate us from his love: neither death, nor life, neither angels nor other heavenly rulers or

powers, neither the present nor the future, neither the world above, nor the world below. There is nothing in all creation that will ever be able to separate us from the love of God which is ours through Christ Jesus our Lord. (Dr. Landry's paraphrase)

I keep the following meaningful words in my Bible.

His safe and radiant Glory,
with rapture they will see,
His wounds will tell the story
to swell the jubilee.[4]

Reflection

The multitudes of people waiting to welcome Gerard made quite an impression on me. It reminds me that all people are equal at death, the small and the great. The grandpa, grandma, or child will be just as valued as a famous preacher, president, or king.

Dr. Landry prefers to use the term *death and return* (D&R) because he feels *near-death experience* (NDE) might not be clearly understood to mean that he was clinically dead. When a doctor who has worked in intensive care for years dies and returns, he knows he was dead.

Dr. Landry says, "I'm so grateful for God's faithfulness for letting me stay on earth nearly two decades more, as of now, to share Jesus' love for the lost." Dr. Landry has spoken and traveled extensively for two international ministries.[5]

There are many messages to consider in Dr. Landry's testimony. Personally, his story has prompted me to delve deeper into the writings of the apostle John. My intensive study has been rich. Many these days believe in physical healing through prayer. They model their beliefs after Jesus' earthly ministry of healing the sick. Yet not too many have made a trip to heaven to be healed and then have returned to tell it! Dr. Landry's heart, lung, and little finger were all healed.

Our Savior showed himself on the cross to give Gerard and us a graphic message. The need for a plan of redemption was no surprise to God. There was already a remedy for Adam's sin. God in his omniscience looked down the corridor of time and saw all that would happen. He saw you and me and in advance planned to meet our needs. He is Alpha and Omega. He knows the beginning from the end. Revelation 13:8 calls Jesus "the Lamb that was slain from the creation of the world." In the past I wondered what that verse meant, as we know Jesus died around two thousand years ago. The Scriptures tell us that Jesus' death was in the divine purpose appointed from the foundation of the world. The book of Genesis was centered in the cross, and the crimson blood of the Lamb of God flows through the entire Bible—to the book of Revelation, and to us today. Through eternity we will praise God for sending his pure and beloved Son to give his life for us. We will praise the Lamb for his love, which caused him to suffer and die for us.

It is also important to remember that Jesus didn't enter heaven again and again like the high priest in the tabernacle or the temple, offering sacrifices for sin. Jesus, the Great High Priest, came to earth to give his life once and for all. He doesn't have to suffer many times but suffered once to do away with sin and the power of sin; this is clearly stated in Hebrews 9:25–28.

The lingering refrain in Landry's message is that "Jesus loves, and he loves, and he loves." It challenges us all to try in our small way to love as God loves.

Healing Prayer

Take a moment to ask how you can be more infused with divine love. What holds you back from receiving more of this gift? Let God put into your mind some loving act of kindness you can do this very day. Find all the Scripture you can on God's love. Mark your Bible and read it at special times of need.

Especially realize that God's Son dearly loves you. Wait in his presence, as Gerry did, to hear Christ speak your name. Perhaps he'll also say your name and "My peace be with you." Remembering his wounds, which tell the story of his love, let his love and peace fill you and bring rest to your soul.

CHAPTER SIX

From Moths to Butterflies

I experienced the reality of the spiritual body and learned that it has every faculty of the physical body, though with greater sensitivity and some dimensions added.... There will be nothing shocking in the transition, only a continuation of who I am now.

Catherine Marshall
The Helper

I met Carolyn McCormick and her husband, Marcus, the same weekend I met Deborah O'Donnell in March 1993. They were attending a healing conference at which I was speaking.[1] In one of my talks I mentioned that I was writing a book on near-death experiences and heaven. After the session Carolyn introduced herself, offering to give me details of her own near-death experience.

Immediately I noted the joy that glowed from her pretty face, which was framed by jet black hair. I learned that she was a registered nurse and mother of four. She was easy to talk to. Yes, I wanted to hear her story.

Carolyn, Marcus, and I managed to squeeze in a half-hour visit over a boxed lunch provided by the conference. We met in the church library, its walls covered with filled mahogany bookcases. As we balanced our lunches on our knees and chatted, I observed the loving relationship between the two. They made an attractive couple, he about a head taller than she.

As the weekend came to a close, I wanted to get Carolyn's story down on tape. A formal interview seemed impossible with the din of friends old and new saying their good-byes. The only place we could find to meet was in a concrete stairwell behind heavy closed doors. Here's the inspiring story I heard.

Angelic Visitation

The details are unimportant, but as a child I was very unhappy. I often wished I'd never been born. I remember one specific day when I was five years old. I was sitting on the swing talking to God, whom I knew personally, and I let him have it! *If I died and went to heaven, I'd let you know there is a better way to run the universe. Living on earth is so painful; there can't be any meaning to it!* That core of anger seemed to define my life even in my young adult years.

In 1966 I was married in a church, which my husband and I rarely attended. My commitment to God had waned. God seemed far removed from our daily life. That was true until 1970 and the birth of our second child.

I had been diagnosed with placenta previa, a condition in which the placenta is implanted low in the uterus, at the cervical opening. It can present a sudden, profuse bleeding. The doctor had induced labor, and on my first contraction I hemorrhaged badly and was rushed to surgery for a C-section. The last thing I remember before going under the anesthetic was two anesthesiologists hovering over my head, arguing. One wanted to put me under, and the other didn't. One felt surgery had to be done immediately; it couldn't wait. The other thought my blood pressure was too low; the surgery might kill me.

The doctor who wanted to anesthetize me won the argument. I "went under." The next thing I recall is "waking up" in a different place. I was no longer in my body, and yet I was myself. I had a body, but it wasn't my earthly body.

Right in front of me stood a rather large angel. I perceived him to be male. He wore a full-length white garment of loose fabric, like a muumuu. No wings. I don't recall seeing his face. His head was covered with a hood, which fell forward, obscuring a face. A bright light seemed to radiate from him.

Behind him, in the distance, was another angel. I had the distinct impression the second angel was observing what the first was doing. It was as if he were a student of the main angel—in training or learning through this process.

I don't remember how or why, but nonverbal communication was happening between the "main" angel and me. There were no words involved; it was more like a mind link, a comprehension beyond human language. I said to him through my thoughts, *Okay, what's this about? You know this can't be right!* I was referring to both my early life and this painful physical disaster.

Reliving My Past with God

In a realm in which time seemed nonexistent, I was allowed to start my life over. Events were chronological, but time didn't exist. I reexperienced my whole life. It wasn't as if I saw my life or was told about it; I was there. I "relived" the same feelings and the same experiences, but this time I was in two places at once. I was a baby or a toddler and was also aware of myself as an adult "looking on" with an angel.

I'll give an example of how it was while reliving my life. When I was three years old, anything that might have happened to me when I was five didn't exist in my consciousness. And I wasn't aware of people I met when I was ten. The review of my childhood could be stopped—put on pause—any time I chose. Then I'd ask the angel—no words, just thoughts—*Okay, why did that happen? Show me why that was necessary or right.*

With each instance, the angel would point out to me the benefits derived from that situation in my own or someone else's life. He showed how it formed my character or helped me grow, how God had used that painful time for something very positive.

Afterward I'd say, *All right, I see. I agree. It's okay that this happened,* and then my life would continue. As I went on, scene after scene, a feeling of extreme love and joy welled up. There was no way I wanted to go back to my body.

But then the angel let me know that I would be returning to my body.

And I refused. *No. I'm not going back there. The earth is too painful. It's a horrible place, and I don't want to go back there. I've had enough! I want to stay here.*

I was emphatic, and yet the angel said, *No, you must go back.* I held my ground. *I'm not going.*

He said, *You will go back,* and then he made me continue with my life's story.

My story progressed to where it was just a year before this current life-threatening birth. (I was not yet aware of this second pregnancy.) I relived the experience of birthing my first child, a beautiful girl whom I loved dearly. When I realized my daughter would be motherless if I didn't "go back," I said, *Yes, you're right. I have to return.* I didn't want her to be raised without a mother's love—without my love.

Yes, I had to go back. But I still negotiated: I wouldn't return to earth unless I was allowed to remember this other-worldly healing experience. I wanted to remember the reasons why everything had happened as it had. I wanted to remember that there was joy at the end of the earthly process I was going through. Going back to my previous limited understanding of my experience was something I definitely did not want.

To remember this new insight, I would have to be given words. Remember, none of this experience involved any words. It was time for me to "go back," and I couldn't seem to find words to hold on to.

The angel told me it was time for me to go, and I said, *No. I won't go until you give me words! I will not go until you give me words!*

Then the angel gave me the words "Moths turn into butterflies," and boom, instantly I was back into my body!

Next thing I knew, I woke up in the hospital room. My husband was with me and asking, "What do you mean, moths turn into butterflies? They don't, you know." Apparently during my time in the recovery room, when the staff asked me my name or anything else, all I would say was, "Moths turn into butterflies." I know now in retrospect that it was because I was so desperately trying to cling to the new understanding I had been given. Not wanting to lose it, I was thoroughly focused on that one phrase.

Seeing that I had regained consciousness, my husband joyfully said, "It's a boy!" We named him Jason.

Over the next few days I asked questions about what had happened to me physically. If my heart stopped beating, I don't know. I do know that because of the extent of the hemorrhaging I had no measurable blood pressure. A whole artery ripped open when the first contraction occurred. It would be like opening your aorta and letting it dump out. It's my guess, with my medical knowledge as a nurse, that I was in this very critical state ten or fifteen minutes. I lost so much blood that I can say I stood at the brink between life and death. I thank God that my son was indeed healthy, not adversely affected.

Because my blood had not been typed and cross-matched, I was not given a transfusion. Now I can say I'm thankful that the blood wasn't ready and that I didn't have a transfusion. My Lord Jesus worked it all out, and I look forward to thanking him face-to-face.

As I regained my health and stamina, I retained the memory—as I've related it—and the phrase. As we all know, moths don't turn into butterflies; caterpillars do. So the statement is a bit of a mystery to me. I feel that the Lord meets us on our own level. When I need to retain knowledge, he gives it to me in pictures and words I can understand. At that point in my life, I was so ignorant of butterflies and moths that I *thought* moths turned into butterflies.

Sometimes I wonder if perhaps the angel said *moths* because our spiritual transformation at death is supernatural, not natural. It is an even more complete transformation than the natural caterpillar-to-butterfly progression. God's realm is something beyond our human vocabulary. It simply doesn't fit into words. There are no words to describe it.

My Healing and Growth

When I "came back," I was like a new person. As I said, I had been angry with God all my life. The anger was gone. I had inner healing. I had also been angry with my parents and siblings and a number of other people. But now I was able to forgive those who had injured me or who I thought had injured me. Months later my husband noted that I didn't seem to get as upset with him as often as I had previously. I tried to explain I now could see life's irritations as temporary and unimportant in the overall picture.

At first I wanted to run around and tell anybody and everybody of my newfound understanding. I thought, *Everybody should have this experience!* It had drained my anger, and it also had removed all of my fear of death. I had no fear anymore because I knew where I was going after my physical death—and who would be with me. However, I was not grounded in Christianity at the time. Because I'd wandered away from the Lord, I had no plumb line.

Through this experience God healed me. As a result I started on a spiritual quest, but it would be a few years before I found biblical explanations, understanding, and a sound relationship with Christ. After my NDE I started reading books, taking an interest in spiritual things, and there I discovered the "humanistic fable." By Eastern religions and the philosophy of Carl Jung, I was fed the humanistic fable that everyone has a heart of pure gold and that the entire human race will not only live forever but will ultimately end up together in heaven. The message I heard here was that we all could relax and do our own thing. The deceiver, Satan, led me off into these and other avenues directed away from God, and great destruction happened because I lacked knowledge of the Bible. My choices led to divorce and years of anxiety and confusion. After six or seven years of this lifestyle, I finally tired of the fruitless search and emptiness and returned to the security of my earlier Christian path.

I would advise anybody who has had a near-death experience or any other supernatural experience to immediately check it out with God's Word and with knowledgeable believers. Make sure you have a strong Christian community so that you will have help putting on the full armor of God, because you will be attacked. When God gives you gifts, Satan wants to remove them.

Twenty-three years after my NDE, its effects have not lessened. I delight each day in the gifts God gives me. The pleasant ones are easy to enjoy, and I have come to value the unpleasant ones as well, because I can see his hand in all the events of my life.

I currently design and make watercolor quilt kits. These kits require more than one hundred different fabrics to make one small wall hanging. Only this large variety of fabrics can result in a Monet-like work. A fewer number of fabrics won't work because the quilt will lack depth and interest. So it has been with me. My Lord has taken all the scraps of my life and assembled them into a beautiful design.

I see life differently now. If I face a difficult situation, I turn to the Scripture verse that says, "In all things God works for the good of those who love him, who have been called according to his purpose" (Rom. 8:28). The angel's message was clear: Any situation I had received with pain could be transformed by the grace of God.

God gave me a beautiful experience I'll never forget. He took me to a heavenly state and healed my soul, then sent me back to earth to help others. I will never be the same.

Reflection

Carolyn and I discussed further the idea that after we die we are entirely new and different creatures with some similarities to our former selves—as moths are similar to butterflies. We will, for instance, recognize one another (1 Cor. 13:12). A caterpillar becoming a butterfly is one creature being changed in form through metamorphosis. This analogy is often used of the new birth in Christ. A moth becoming a butterfly may well be more descriptive of this transformation at death.

The *Living Bible* puts it this way: "The Scriptures tell us that the first man, Adam, was given a natural, human body, but Christ is more than that, for he was life-giving Spirit. First, then, we have these human bodies and later on God gives us spiritual, heavenly bodies. Adam was made from the dust of the earth, but Christ came from heaven above. Every human being has a body just like Adam's, made of dust, but all who become Christ's will have the same kind of body as his—a body from heaven" (1 Cor. 15:45–48).

Resurrection is great to look forward to. Our new-birth experience is a foretaste of it. In fact, it's called the earnest money on that which we will one day receive in full (Eph. 1:13–14).

You may not have an angelic encounter like Carolyn, but you can still walk back through your life with Jesus by his Holy Spirit. Looking at your life's hurts through God's eyes changes everything. Don't look at the past except with Christ and his unconditional love for you. Journal what healings you receive. Pray with someone else if you need further help.

Healing Prayer

Take a quiet moment, open your hands in surrender, and offer to our healing Christ all the clashing events of your past and present. Tell him they are too big for you, too overwhelming. Give the great Weaver the soft fabrics of silken ice blue, creamy pink, pure holy white, lemon yellow, strands of glowing silver and shining gold. Try not to be tense. Breathe deeply. Allow him to work. Yes, give him also the burlap of dull gray, plain taupes, and earthen tans and browns. Relax a little more deeply into his loving arms. Now let go of the rough fabric of angry red, bitter orange, and shocking black. His loving arms surround you. Release. Rest.

All of these fabrics and colors represent a hundred others. He, better than any earthly artist, will pull it all together into an exquisite design, a work of art beyond price. You won't see all the results now. Think of it as a great work of art: Sometimes you must stand away from it to see it best. Without any dark places it would look unbalanced and bland. The true picture can be seen only through him and with him by your side. You will admire it eventually. Perhaps you've already begun to admire it—and you will all the more in the ages to come.

Trust him. It will happen. It is happening.

CHAPTER SEVEN

A Bridge to the Other Side

*You have delivered my soul from death
    and my feet from stumbling,
that I may walk before God
    in the light of life.*

King David
Psalm 56:13

———•———

Pam Johnstone dresses attractively and carries herself well, as someone you'd expect to be in a managerial position. In fact, that's what she is—assistant manager of a Seattle bank. When you meet Pam, you note one main quality—her calm, peaceful air. Her warm blue eyes reflect this peace. Perhaps this calmness came through an experience she had earlier in life as well as her active faith since her teenage years.

I met her first at St. Alban's Church and more personally as we socialized with mutual friends. In 1990 Pam told me of an experience that happened while she was undergoing surgery in 1971. When Pam was twenty-three, before her second son was born, her husband, Brian, was in language school at a military base in California, and Pam, at home, began having severe stomach pains. Doctors couldn't identify the problem. She seemed too young to be having gall bladder attacks, so the doctors on her case did not give that serious consideration. But the pain persisted and surgery was scheduled. Here's Pam's story.

Wanting to Cross Over

I just wanted to die. I didn't want to feel the pain any longer. Childbirth with my first child was nothing compared to this pain.

77

Besides, you know labor pains will end, and you know why you're in pain. But in this case we didn't know what the trouble was.

Heavy pain medication had been given to me some time before the surgery. At 11:00 A.M. I was put under anesthesia for the two-hour operation itself, and I went into deeper than normal sleep.

Sometime during the surgery or in the recovery room, I felt I had "awakened" in a place other than the hospital or my home. I guess I'd say I was cognizant of all my senses. Being aware that the physical pain was gone felt wonderful. A nice cool breeze blew on me—like when you're driving in the car with the window down. The temperature was perfect. There was peace and an all-over comfort you could never even imagine. The lightness and calmness I felt are hard to describe. I remember a bright light, like sunlight on a sunny afternoon when you'd normally need sunglasses—or like the reflection that comes off a body of water. But I didn't feel I needed sunglasses for protection. This light didn't hurt my eyes.

The next thing I remember was walking and looking around trying to figure out where I was. I was in something like a green meadow. Walking was easy there; it was more like flowing than walking. I found myself nearing a bridge. Then I stepped higher to the footpath of the bridge.

When I stepped onto the bridge, I saw someone ahead of me about halfway across. The light was shining behind the person, maybe coming from the garments. I kept walking, trying to make out who the person was. Then as I walked farther on the bridge, he (or she; I couldn't tell) put his hand onto the bridge rail in front of me to prevent my crossing.

I said, "I want to cross over." I put my hand on his to push it away. Looking up at his face, I still saw only a very bright light and couldn't make out his features.

I said again, "I want to get to the other side."

A very soothing voice responded, "It's not your time."

"I don't care what time it is," I said. "I'm not going to feel this kind of pain anymore!"

He said, "You will not feel this kind of pain anymore. You have to go back; you're still needed there."

The next thing I knew, I heard Brian's voice calling me, "Pam! Pam!" When I awoke at seven that evening, I saw the doctor, nurses, and my husband all standing around my bed. They all seemed relieved and said I could go back to sleep.

Why are they trying so hard to wake me and then, in the next breath, telling me to go back to sleep? I wondered.

When I woke again the next day, the doctors came in and told me they had tried to awaken me all day. They thought I was going into a coma, which I might not have come out of. They had been ready to call my father (we were very close) to fly down from Seattle to see if his voice could rouse me.

I told my doctor, the resident who was in charge of the case and who had assisted in the surgery, about the kind of "dream experience" I had had while under anesthesia. When I asked him if he believed in a world beyond this, he responded by saying that he was a Christian and he believed I had had a near-death experience.

"When you came back," he said, "you had a presence, alertness, and puzzled awareness not normal for people coming out of a semicoma."

The surgery had revealed a nonfunctioning gall bladder, which the surgeon removed. My husband had suspected this to be the problem all along, because gall bladder trouble was prevalent in my family. Although I was in ICU no heart monitor was tracking me, so we have no medical proof that my heart stopped or for how long. However, my doctor himself referred to my near-death experience.

Reflection

When I asked Pam how she felt about death, she responded, "I haven't been afraid of it. . . . The only regret I'd have would be leaving my family and other loved ones behind. I can't explain it, but it's not something I fear. My experience also gave me a feeling of purpose and a deep peace inside."

I enjoyed Pam's description of the heavenly breezes being like driving in the car with your window down on a sunny day. The sunlight is bright, but it doesn't hurt your eyes. And this was only the outskirts of heaven. C. S. Lewis, in *The Last Battle*, talks about going "further up and further in," things getting better and better.

I look forward to walking through—or floating through—Eden-like lush green meadows. Hawaii and Jamaica are great places to visit, but her description sounds better than any vacation spot I've been to. What do you think?

Healing Prayer

Have you lost someone who crossed over to the other side? Are you in pain about it? If so, will you take a moment to speak to God about your feelings? God took Pam's physical pain away from her, and he wants to take your emotional pain away too. Tell God honestly if you can't carry the pain any longer. His brilliance and glory is shining on you as it did on Pam. Listen to what our healing Lord Jesus says. Write down your feelings and what you hear in your heart. Know that God cares. Wait in his presence. If you need more help, talk to a person who knows how to pray for emotional healing or to a counselor.

CHAPTER EIGHT

Escape from the River of Death

You'd have to be the greatest pessimist in the world to believe that life beyond this is a lesser experience.

Lester Sauvage, heart surgeon
interview

———◆———

For years no one in Seattle could compete with Lorraine Tutmarc for "best Christmas decorations." Every year for about ten years the *Seattle Times* awarded Lorraine the prize for the exquisite decorating of her home. Finally, after receiving so many accolades, she asked the *Times* to share the awards with other contestants.

Lights decked all the trees outside her house, and she decorated seven trees inside. Colored, blinking lights lined the house, the windows, and even the roof. At one window Lorraine set thirty-five beautifully dressed dolls representing different countries. The carport held a manger scene with biblical characters made from dressmaker forms. Animals were cut from plywood and realistically painted. Public transport buses came by, sometimes until 1:00 A.M., to show off the house of "the Christmas lady."

When I met Lorraine in the spring of 1992, she was eighty-six years old. She was one of three people I interviewed on KTBW-TBN in Federal Way, Washington. She was a most responsive and vivacious interview subject, telling me about her near-death experience. Her son Bud accompanied her.

Bud sent me a booklet of his mother's poems, many of which were obviously inspired by her near-death experience. The booklet also includes a drawing in which she depicts that experience. A photo of Lorraine as a young woman shows that she had been a stately brunette beauty, five-foot-nine. Bud tells me she loved long dresses and coats with fur collars.

Lorraine and her husband raised two children, a boy and a girl. She was a capable real estate salesperson.

Lorraine died in 1992. To write her story below, I relied on my 1992 television interview, subsequent phone conversations with those who knew her, and a taped 1987 interview by a pastor friend, Ruben Korpi, of Seattle.[1] On this tape Pastor Korpi says of Lorraine, "I always rejoice in her testimony, no matter how often I've heard it. I've known Lorraine forty-five years, so my friendship with her and her family goes way back." Here is Lorraine's story.

Sent Home to Die

I do believe in miracles. Birth is a miracle. Death is a miracle. It's all a part of life, which is a miracle. I do believe in life after death. *Everything in life leads to the day we're going to go to be with God, forever and forever.*

From childhood days I've always believed in Jesus and in God. I would say a prayer when I went to bed at night. I loved to think of him even when I would pick flowers. All the wonderful things he created were very interesting to me. Yet I'd never had the experience of salvation. I didn't realize there was a personal experience like that, nor did I read the Bible.

But then I had my near-death experience. I was twenty-two years old and pregnant with my third child. Because of peritonitis and blood poisoning, my baby died. There was nothing the medics could do for me, because there were no antibiotics then. This was in the spring of 1928.

I had been in the hospital three times, and now the doctor had sent me home, telling me nothing more could be done for me. I'd really been sent home to die. My life was being sustained through intravenous feedings. Every time the doctor came into our home, I would hear him ask my husband in a voice that was far too loud, "Has she gone yet?" For about three months I had pain throughout my body and was almost too weak to move.

Lying there on the bed one morning, I realized the pain had left my body. I wasn't thinking of anything, just looking up toward the ceiling, when I felt something strange happen. It felt like I was lifted out of my body, and I went right to the upper corner of the room, where I'd been looking.

Experiencing Eternity

As I rose to the ceiling, I looked back. My husband, the doctor, and a nurse were gathered around my bed. I thought, *Now, that's funny,* because I could see myself—my body—lying on the bed sleeping. Yet here I was, floating and euphoric with peace. I remember asking myself, *How did I do this?*

Then I moved backward, going through the wall. Immediately I found myself up to my neck in a black river, black as black could be, and very cold. My physical pain, absent moments before, had returned. The water was whirling around me. In my mind I asked, *Where am I?*

I heard a loud, loving voice say, "This is eternity. This is eternity. You are lost!" It echoed, "You are lost!" The strong voice came from behind me, so I didn't *see* who it was, but I knew it was God's voice.

What is this? I again asked in my mind.

He replied, "This is the River of Death." His voice echoed, "This is the River of Death."

I didn't know what "being lost" or what a "river of death" was all about. Jesus as Savior was unknown to me at this time. When I was three or four years old, I had started going to Sunday school with my sister and brother. I liked going to the children's activities, but we didn't learn anything like salvation. And I hadn't been to church since I was young.

I had terrible fear when I was enveloped by that black water; I can't swim. When I saw all that water, I knew I was dying. And when this voice told me I was lost and this was eternity, then I knew God was revealing to me my lost condition. I started swirling around in this water, which became like a whirlpool. It kept on going around and around, faster and faster and faster, dragging me under. I was fighting to save my life. In pain, misery, and fear, I kept sinking down into this water. When I got down to the bottom, I couldn't fight anymore. Completely exhausted, I gave up.

Then I saw light enter the water around me. The water turned warm. I looked up at the light and saw Jesus about four feet above me in an opening over my head. Everything else was black, but he was brilliant! The light coming from him was beyond description. His hair was an auburn color and wavy. He looked down at me. He had such beautiful eyes. I'll never forget those eyes. They were so large and full of meaning—and kindness and forgiveness and compassion. *Everything you would want to see in Jesus' face was there.*

I had to know I was lost before I could be saved. He had such a compassionate face. I'll never forget that. Yet Jesus was not smiling, but sad. His eyes were so penetrating.

When looking at his pale ivory robe, I saw a big blotch of red on his chest and wondered what it meant. I couldn't see what it was and was curious to figure it out. It was just a big blotch.

Rescued and Healed

Instantly a voice spoke. Though I hadn't asked, he knew what I wanted to know! He said, "This is the blood that I shed on the cross for your sins." I understood his meaning: I knew I was in the wrong as the blood was explained to me.

Then Jesus said, "Follow me."

I said, "I will!"

The minute I said, "I will," the water was gone. He had put his right hand down in the water, and when he said, "Follow me," all the darkness was gone out of my life, gone completely! A brilliance, but it wasn't sunshine, came from Jesus. A transparent gold light came from him, from his body.

When I reached up with my left hand and took hold of his warm hand, I instantly felt the power of God come through my body. I had never heard of the power of God. Later I would use words from a hymn to describe the feeling of God's power. It was like "sparks from smitten steel" coming right through my body from my head to my toes again and again. I grew stronger and stronger as the power went through me!

Finally I thought, *I'm well. I have no more pain. This is real! This is real!*

When I said, *It's real*, I looked up to Jesus. All he had said was, "Follow me." *That's all he would have to say to anybody!*

A Heavenly Visit and Return

Both of us seemed to float toward a wall. We stopped perhaps fifteen feet away from the wall. I was still holding his hand, and I followed his gaze. He was looking straight ahead. I looked up and saw a transparent wall, shining like pure gold, as far as I could see in either direction.[2] I could see into it, eight inches or more, but not all the way through. Oh, I wanted to see behind that wall.

From behind the wall I heard much activity. Everything was alive behind that wall. It seemed like the dawn of a new day; day was just breaking! It was a beautiful experience. I heard little birds singing, tiny birds, and they got louder and louder. People have said there are no birds in heaven, but I heard them.

Then I heard what seemed like millions of little golden bells ringing, tinkling; they rang and rang. Many times since, I've heard those bells in the middle of the night. (And it's not high blood pressure doing that!) Next I heard humming and then a choir singing. The singing got louder and louder, and it was in a minor key. It was beautiful and in perfect harmony. I also heard stringed instruments.

I knew there were flowers. I could smell them but couldn't see them. Their fragrance was like perfume on a gentle breeze— a very gentle breeze.

Then, because the light was so brilliant, it seemed to be getting around noontime. I stepped forward to search for a gate but didn't see any. It just wasn't time for me to go in there yet.

I turned around to look at Jesus, but he was gone. I didn't see him go or hear him go. He was just gone! Then in an instant or so, I felt myself in my body and back in bed.

I never wanted to come back here, I thought. *I was looking for the gates to heaven.*

My desire is to go back and see the rest of it. I'm sure it's much more beautiful than what I saw, because I wasn't there long enough. It's just like what Revelation 22 says about the beautiful things in heaven, but I'd never read that passage! I'd never read anything of this nature before my experience.

When I came back into my body, my husband, Paul, was standing there, leaning over me, holding his hands. He wasn't praying, I know, because he didn't pray then, but he was holding his hands. He was so anxious.

I opened my eyes and said, "I've seen the Lord. I've seen the Lord." I kept on saying it.

Trying to calm me, Paul said, "Rest. Try to close your eyes, and try to rest now. Rest."

I said: "You don't understand; I've seen the Lord."

The doctor and his nurse were there. I was so hungry. It was springtime, so I asked them for asparagus, tea, and toast. I wanted everything to function just as if I were well.

Despite protests from the doctor, the nurse finally brought me food only because I kept asking for it. The medical team wasn't confident that I'd be able to eat.

Oh, it tasted good! I ate it all with no negative results and I asked for seconds. They wouldn't give me any. There was no second helping, and no dessert!

Then I said, "How long am I going to have to be in bed?"

The doctor looked at me funny—to think that I thought I was healed! He could hardly believe it.

He said, "You'd better stay there awhile yet."

But when the nurse and doctor went out of the room, I would get over to the edge of the bed and put my foot down on the floor. I would try to strengthen my feet. I would have tried to get up if they would have allowed me to.

My doctor had an interesting reaction to my physical healing. I heard him later on say to his nurse, *"I have been an atheist, but now I've seen a miracle."*

My Family Changed Too

When I came back from near death, I was different. I didn't feel I belonged here. I don't know how much time my near-death experience took. All I know is that when I left the room, I was dying; when I came back, I was well. There was new life in me.

When I was released from my doctor's care, my housekeeper stayed on to help me. Of course my husband, Paul, and Jeanne and Bud, my little girl and boy, were there. I didn't want to stay in bed. I wanted to get going. I had to gain a little strength. But just think, in about two weeks time, I started painting inside my house.

My husband was just spellbound by it all. Before this he had always wanted to talk about music. Now every time he met somebody or someone came to our house, he'd tell about his wife's experience.

My near-death experience changed the whole course of my life. For one thing, my interests changed. My husband was a theatrical man, a musician, and he had friends who did not go to church. He did quite a bit of entertaining at the time. He'd have his company come, and though he was happy about my NDE and healing, he was very unhappy about the way I acted.

Paul said, "You're just like a wallflower. You aren't one of us anymore."

Of course, I couldn't be like them. I didn't want or like anything they did. Nothing.

The difference in my life was from night to day. It was as though I'd died and gone on.

I knew what I believed, but there were no Christians around me. I didn't really know what to do to connect myself with a group of Christians.

I used to pray for my husband, and I'd pray that he'd have a deep faith, as I now had.

He was building electric guitars and needed some extra help crafting the woodwork on the guitars.[3] He contacted a man down in the south end who did beautiful woodwork. That was an answer to prayer, because the man, Emerald Baunsgard, and his wife started praying for Paul.

We eventually went to church at Hollywood Temple (now Calvary Temple). The second time we attended, during an altar call, my daughter, my son, my husband, and myself, all went to the altar to commit our lives to God.

I've had some wonderful things happen since then. In fact, I had prayed that God would never let me die until everyone in my family got saved, and everyone now so far has been saved. [At the time of her death Lorraine had eight grandchildren, seven great-grandchildren, and five great-great-grandchildren.]

Reflection

On December 19, 1992, Lorraine had a chance to go back and see what was behind the beautiful wall. Although she's gone now, her message of hope is still here. Of all the many inspiring thoughts in Lorraine's story, the wall that encircles the heavenly city of God stands out to me. It must be a glorious and fascinating piece of architecture. In part 3 we will look in detail at this wall as it is described in the book of Revelation.

Lorraine's true story brings up the subject of choosing eternal fellowship or separation from God. Standing at the brink between life and death, she was given a chance to say yes or no to God.

Some people claim that everyone will go to heaven. But in Luke's gospel we hear Jesus himself warning of a hell to avoid (16:19–31). Luke also tells of two thieves who were crucified alongside Jesus. Facing death, one thief chose to be with Jesus in paradise while the other cursed him and was separated from God for eternity (23:39–43).

In my research for this book, I found only one man, Richard Eby, M.D., who experienced both heaven and hell. He tells about this in his autobiography, *Caught Up into Paradise*.[4] In a NDE resulting from a serious accident, falling headfirst off a sundeck, Dr. Eby experienced heaven. Later God gave him a supernatural vision (not NDE) through which he experienced hell. His two opposite experiences gave him quite a complete viewpoint, and he feels called to warn people to escape hell.[5]

The choice—to say yes or no to Jesus Christ, the Light of the World—has to be made in this one and only life, even if it is with the person's last breath. Since Jesus' death and resurrection, there are no second chances. Lorraine's story and others indicate that in the final seconds of life people may have a chance to make this choice.

A confirming Scripture is Jesus' parable of the workers in the vineyard—those who came to the vineyard last received the same wage as those who came early in the day (Matt. 20:1–16). Toward the end of this story about the Kingdom of God, the full-day vineyard workers are complaining: "These men who were hired last worked only one hour, and you have made them equal to us who have borne the burden of the work and the heat of the day." The landowner answered one of them, "Friend, I am not being unfair to you. Didn't you agree to work for a denarius [a day's wage]? Take your pay and go. I want to give the man who was hired last the same as I gave you" (see vv. 12–14). This is the kind of generous person Jesus Christ is; he will accept a person who says yes to him even in the dying breath.

I don't advocate waiting to the end to make this decision. It's far too risky. Besides, those who wait miss out on fellowship with God and the peace and joy that he gives in the present.

Healing Prayer

Do you feel that you are separated from God's presence? Then reach out and take Jesus' hand. He's reaching out to you, too. Say something like, "Jesus Christ, come and save me." He'll take you by your hand to lift you out of whatever kind of black river you're in—whether it's one of loneliness, despair, or lostness. Take some time to talk to God about your own need for rescue.

If you've never been rescued from unbelief in Jesus Christ as the resurrected Son of God, he wants to rescue you now. After he pulled Lorraine out of the River of Death, he said, "Follow me." He alone can give you eternal life. Will you tell him that you receive him as Savior from eternal death and as Giver of eternal life? After you do this, take a deep breath of his resurrection life and wait in his presence. Thank him for these gifts of a lifetime. Never, never stop thanking him.

Paul's letter to the Colossians says it well—for Lorraine and for all of us: "He has rescued us out of the darkness and gloom of Satan's kingdom and brought us into the kingdom of his dear Son, who bought our freedom with his blood and forgave us all our sins" (1:13–14 TLB).

CHAPTER NINE

Tug-of-War for My Soul

*Life is short and we have never too much time for gladden-
ing the hearts of those who are traveling . . . with us. Oh, be
swift to love, make haste to be kind.*

Henri Frederick Amiel
Acts of Kindness

———— ✦ ————

In 1992 some longtime friends, Andy Schuster and his sister
Christine Khemis, invited me to a dinner and evening gathering.
And there I met Craig Gottschalk, a six-foot-five, good-looking
man in his mid thirties, with short-trimmed hair. (Interestingly,
Craig is the grandson of Lorraine Tutmarc, whose story you just
read in chapter 8. It is undoubtedly rare for two relatives to each
have an NDE.) Over delicious chicken tacos, I discovered that
Craig had a fascinating near-death experience. I, who then had
been a widow only a short time, encouraged Craig to tell his story
to the whole group.

I usually carry a pen and notepad with me, but this evening I
wasn't properly outfitted. Of course, I didn't know that I was going
to need them. I'm grateful that someone taped Craig's story. What
follows is his heaven-and-back experience, which took place on
June 1, 1976.

Drugged Out

What happened to me when I was eighteen was what the
apostle Paul probably would have called a vision.[1] Today it would
be called a near-death experience.

I grew up in what many people might call a Christian home. We went to church one hour a week but not every week. The idea of having a personal relationship with God was foreign to me. I was not really born again; I had never truly given my heart to Jesus Christ, accepting the salvation he had for me. When I was in my middle teen years, my parents got divorced. My father moved away, and I didn't get to see him anymore. My mother was working all the time trying to support us three children.

I got in with the wrong group of kids and started doing drugs. I wore my hair down to my shoulders like the rest of the guys. Smoking pot and drinking were daily occurrences for me. I also did hard drugs—acid, coke, heroin, you name it—including THC. Of all these chemicals, I leaned most toward hallucinogens. When I moved out of my mother's home, I lived with four or five other people who had similar lifestyles.

I was a high school dropout, and I lived like a bum. One night when I was eighteen, a bunch of people came over for a party. We had saved up so that we could buy a big cache of drugs for that night. We made a cocktail of many different drugs, and we all got high. I was ready to pass out. I remember seeing, as I stumbled into my room, my digital clock as it flashed 1:00 A.M. Then I fell on my bed and passed out.

Life's Video

The next thing I knew I was stone-cold sober, wide awake, standing before God, my judge.[2] It is said that when people die, their lives flash before their eyes; they see their whole lives in panoramic view. This is true of many who have been in bad car accidents, have nearly drowned, or have had other close calls. And it is exactly what happened to me. My life was played back for me to watch like a video. Every sin I had committed from childhood to the time I was eighteen had been recorded and now was being played back. When you're standing there in front of God, watching your life, you don't have anything to say to defend yourself. You can't argue or deny it. You're just there watching what you did, every bit of it. Viewing my whole life seemed to take a long time. When we got to the last day, it was the end of my life. In the review of my life history, there wasn't any place where I had accepted Jesus Christ for salvation, so I was pronounced guilty and sentenced to hell.

Revelation 20:13–15 says: "I saw the dead, small and great, standing before God, and books were opened. And another book was opened, which is the Book of Life. And the dead were judged according to their works, by the things which were written in the books. . . . Anyone not found written in the Book of Life was cast into the lake of fire" (NKJV). The lake of fire was where I started to go. I didn't like this judgment or the thought that I would have to go to hell. And yet I was kind of at peace with it because I knew it was the right thing. I knew it had to happen. It was a just decision. When you sit and watch everything you've done in your whole life recorded accurately, then you know, *Yes, I am guilty. I'm caught.*

Experiencing the Pains of Hell

So off I went. It was as if I were falling toward this place. At first it wasn't so bad, but then I started to feel the torment little by little. I began feeling the pain that goes on there.

This is what it was like for me: It wasn't like burning up in a fire, but it was a sense of guilt and shame that was so strong it hurt. Have you ever lost someone or felt so guilty, so bad about it, that the emotion hurt? That is what hell was like—but the pain there was so much stronger; it is on a much greater level than we will ever experience here. It can't be adequately described.

When it got close to the point where I couldn't stand it anymore, I started screaming, "Forgive me; save me from this pain." It kept getting worse—and worse. I screamed louder—and louder. The torment was real! Finally Jesus came, took hold of me, and started pulling me back. When he pulled me back, the torment subsided. The farther away I got, the less it hurt.

Then Satan showed up and said: "Wait a minute! You can't have him; he belongs to me. He's mine. Let go!"

The following psalm is an accurate description of what happened to me: "The sorrows of death compassed me, and the pains of hell got hold of me: I found trouble and sorrow. Then I called upon the name of the Lord: O Lord, I beseech you, deliver my soul.

Gracious is the Lord, and righteous; yes, our God is merciful. The Lord preserves the simple: I was brought low, and he helped me" (Ps. 116:3–6, my paraphrase).

On the television series, *L.A. Law*, the lawyers try to put together a case on why a person is guilty. That's what Satan did. He put together the things that I had done, and what I hadn't done, and why Jesus couldn't have me. When Satan said I belonged to him, he was accusing me. He reiterated and confirmed all the things I had just been shown and convicted of; he stood there making a legal argument against me.[3] Satan pulled me back with him, and as I was drawn back, I felt the torment and started screaming again.

Then a tug-of-war started, with Jesus on one side and Satan on the other. I went through several cycles of being pulled back and forth. When Jesus was winning, I praised him and yelled, "Yeah!" When Satan was winning, I was screaming, "Help me!" Finally, after several times of going back and forth, Jesus pulled me out of there. He said he was going to save me because of *my grandmother's constant prayers.* She had been praying for me for the eighteen years of my life. (This was my grandma Tutmarc.)

Heaven's Stairway

After that, Jesus showed me a stairway. He used this stairway to teach me two things. First, that God is eternal. He took me down it for a long way and up it for a long way. He showed me that no matter how far we went down, we would not be any closer to the beginning of it. And no matter how far we went up, we would not be any closer to the top. I could see no end in either direction. There is no first step and no last step to that stairway. There is no creation of God. God always has been, and God always will be. He is the Alpha and Omega, the first and the last, the beginning and the end.[4]

The second stairway lesson was about God's wisdom. Picture a stairway: There's a top and a front to every step. On the front of every step was written, in red letters or numbers, a sentence or a formula—some knowledge, an equation, something scientific. On the front of every step was written a piece of God's knowledge. Again, there was no end to the steps, as there is no end to his knowledge. The Scriptures say, "By wisdom the LORD laid the earth's foundations, by understanding he set the heavens in place; by his knowledge the deeps were divided" (Prov. 3:19–20). His knowledge is so amazing. He made the earth out of his knowledge.

Even if you could understand everything in the universe, there are still millions of other aspects of God's knowledge and wisdom. "He knows infinitely" is the only way to describe it. He has infinite power and infinite knowledge. I try not to say, "God knows everything and can do everything," but instead, "God is infinite and he knows infinitely."

Experiencing Heaven and Angels

Then in the next part of my experience I was taken to heaven, where there was an extremely large room, so big it was beyond the limits of what I could see. Behind me were the Book of Life and the Lord. In front of me were tens of thousands, millions of angels, all standing in perfect silence, almost at attention, waiting reverently for the ceremony to begin. I was very nervous standing before a million or so angels looking at me with such concentration.

Jesus introduced me by my spiritual name; I can't remember what it was, but it wasn't Craig. I remember he called me a name I knew and recognized as my own. My name was ceremoniously written in the Book of Life. Which name was written, earthly or heavenly, I do not know, since I was facing the other direction. And then the celebration of angels began. The angels' rejoicing over salvation is found in Luke: "There is rejoicing in the presence of the angels of God over one sinner who repents" (15:10).

The angels started singing and praising, much as we do here on earth at times. It sounded like a perfect orchestra, yet they were all doing their own thing. It all blended into great harmony. It was beautiful, an incredible sound, and it went on for a long time. I just stood and watched in awe at this heavenly celebration over my name being written in the Book of Life.

These angels didn't have wings. They had real and solid bodies but not like ours. You could see through them—or into them—for a quarter to half an inch. You could see through a little bit on the edge—like through their "skin"—but you couldn't see through the solid center part. They seemed very tall, but I didn't have anything to gauge it by. They weren't male or female but had characteristics of both. They seemed both male and female and yet neither.

Sent Back for a Mission

After all these experiences, Jesus took me out of the room. It became darker. He said, "I'm going to send you back because I have work for you to do." The last thing he said to me before sending me back was "Breathe."[5]

When he told me to breathe, I was back in my body, awake. There was no air in me. I felt as if I'd had the wind knocked out of me. If you've ever had the unpleasant experience of being winded, that first breath is a tough one; I expect that's what a baby's first breath is like. When I took my first breath, that was when I was born again.

Remember, I had looked at the clock in my room before I'd passed out. It had just turned 1:00. Now it said 1:45. I had been "gone" for forty-five minutes. Normally with the drugs I had taken just before 1:00, I would have been out, unconscious, from four to six hours. Even if I could have awakened in a shorter time, I could not have walked without stumbling or talked coherently. Yet I stood right up, packed my things, and went out to my car—a '66 GTO. In fact, I now sensed God telling me to get out of there—immediately. My car, which normally got about five miles per gallon, was out of gas. It had run out of gas just up the street earlier that day, and I had coasted to the driveway. I had intended to get a ride to the gas station the next day.

But here, in the middle of the night, I hopped in the car. To my amazement the engine started right up. I drove about thirty miles with no gas! By the time I got to my destination—my mother's house—it was 2:30 in the morning. I knocked on the door, waking my mother and stepfather.

My mother said, "Craig, what are you doing here? What's wrong?" Obviously, if it's 2:30 in the morning and someone knocks on the door, there's a problem.

I told my parents, "You won't believe what's happened to me!" I told them everything that had taken place a few hours before. My incredible story left them wondering what to make of it all. They took me in, and that day my life changed forever.

I never touched drugs again. No getting drunk, no pot, no coke, no drugs. I'm delivered from all those habits. I came back a different person.

Future Plans

Craig told me that he even celebrates his birthday on June 1 rather than on his biological birthday. He said, "My actual birthday doesn't count, because I died physically; I was raised up spiritually and physically from death." June 1 is now his combined physical and spiritual birthday.

"My desire is to totally live for God," Craig told me in a later phone conversation. Since I first met him, he has worked toward a dream of becoming a missionary pilot. In 1993 he became a commercial pilot. In 1994 he got his multiengine rating. In 1995 he became an aviation mechanic. He completed Seattle Bible College in August 1995, and his heart's desire is to serve his Lord as a missionary pilot.

Reflection

In Craig's story he himself gives some reflection of what his experience meant. In closing, I note that I am struck by three things in particular. First, Craig's is an encouraging example to remind us that grandparents' and parents' prayers are powerful. Such intercessory prayers often help break the power of demonic influences. So keep praying!

Second, because Craig returned to his body, his salvation was assured and he was then able to live a new life. Craig was skating too close to the edge of eternity. He said that when he took his first breath, that was when he was born again. His ending could have been very different. One shudders to think about it.

My third comment is about the beautiful stairway showing the unfathomable wisdom God offers. This picture is such a contrast from Craig's life of drugs. It was as if God was saying to Craig, and to all of us, *I have so many treasures of incredible wisdom for you. Why do you choose to go after the world's destructive, alluring temptations? You could be having the best, but instead you've chosen shallow, fleeting, and empty things.*

Not everyone has a second chance as Craig did. I'm so glad he chose to tell us his story.

Healing Prayer

Did one person or several people pray for you to help bring you to a place of faith? Was one a grandparent or a parent? Take a moment to thank God for all these caring people.

Are you praying for a child or grandchild? The prayer connection, especially between a mother and child, is powerful. Mothers often seem to know intuitively when a child is in trouble. Be encouraged to know that God and his angels are taking note of your prayers. Lift up your loved ones every time God brings them to mind as well as in regular times of intercession.

Take time right now to pray. It may look impossible, but remember Craig and don't give up. You will be rewarded someday. Thank God for his limitless wisdom and knowledge. Colossians 2:3 (Phillips) says, "For it is in him, and in him alone, that men will find all the treasures of wisdom and knowledge." Standing at the base of the ladder, Craig saw that there was no end to either the ladder or God's wisdom. God will give you the wisdom you need for school, your family, your job—whatever your need may be. Ask God. Study the Scriptures. His storehouse of knowledge is endless.

Now, relax and pray, waiting in his presence.

PART THREE

Let It Be
for
Ecstasy

CHAPTER TEN

Wonders of the Heavenly City

They knew that they were pilgrims and strangers here below, and looked not much on these things, but lifted their eyes up to Heaven their dearest country, where God has prepared for them a city.

William Bradford
Plymouth Plantation

———◆———

You have heard inspiring descriptions of heaven from seven witnesses. Several of these men and women had little biblical background, and yet these twentieth-century stories have the ring of the ancient words of Scripture. Since none of these men and women remained in their heavenly state, they didn't get as far in as we will in this chapter through the avenue of Scripture. Here we will explore the interior of heaven. In this context you will also see, interwoven here and there, a few of my experiences in earthly Jerusalem. But before we proceed with that, I want to tell you about an experience my mother had at my birth.

My mother, Loretta Jesse Reed, nearly died when I was born. I was her fourth and last child. Physically she was quite overweight and not in the best of health. Ever since I could remember, she'd had a heart condition. Perhaps her heart stopped for a short period, or she may have hemorrhaged at my birth.

She was not well at the time, but I was. I was born looking like a plump little doll with rows of fat adorning my legs, arms, and waist. Funny that I turned out to be the smallest in the family, but I weighed in at nearly ten pounds. One could say I was a silver-dollar baby. My dad filled two wooden cigar boxes with silver dollars he collected at his store. He nailed the boxes shut and gave them as payment to the doctor who delivered me.

As I grew up, occasionally my mother's warm brown eyes would look into mine and she would say, "Rita, when you were born, I went to heaven to get you."

What a healing thing for her to say to me. Mom, who had a quiet and gentle soul, would then mention the streets of gold and pearly gates. She'd say, "When I was in heaven I didn't want to come back because it was so wonderful. But God sent me back to my family."

Throughout my childhood I'd try to picture what heaven was like and wonder about it all. As a teenager I'd sometimes think maybe my mother's experience was just a dream. In time, I rarely thought about it.

Little did she or I imagine that I would one day be writing a book about people who had near-death experiences. But only well after her death in 1967 did I consider the possibly that my mother may have had an NDE. The term *near-death experience* was not coined at that time, and such happenings were rarely discussed. My brother, Dr. Bob Reed, D.D.S, nine years my senior, thinks I may be right, as he also remembers Mom's saying that she had died and gone to "another dimension."

In the early 1980s some friends, Shade and Janet, were praying with me. One of them said, "When your mother experienced heaven you were still attached to her by the umbilical cord, so you probably had a touch of heaven right along with her." What a thought to ponder! Since then my mother's words have taken on a new interest for me.

Whether I shared my mother's experience of heaven, I don't know. Yet some have wondered at the inner strength I have exhibited since childhood. Maybe a taste of heaven at my birth added to my most important experience—my new birth in Christ, entering a personal relationship with Jesus when I was nine years old, followed by baptism.

My mother, a strong Christian, in her seventieth year had a chance to revisit those streets of gold. It gives me comfort to know she's now with her Lord.

I don't know if you believe in heaven and golden streets, but since you've stayed with me this long, perhaps you're hoping it's true. Those of you who believe may be looking for encouragement, eager to learn more about the heavenly destination of you or your loved ones.

What Is Heaven?

Opinions on the subject of heaven vary. Some with a non-biblical opinion may say, "Heaven is what you make it here on earth." Some will say poetic things like "Heaven is in a flower or a sunset." Among Christians—Gentile and Jewish believers—there are also different opinions of what Scripture confirms about heaven. Some will accept only the accounts of the Gospels and Epistles. Others add the Old Testament Scriptures, and some accept the entire Bible including its last book, Revelation. *To Heaven and Back* reflects this last category.

Jesus describes a specific place prepared for the children of God: "In my Father's house are many mansions: if it were not so, I would have told you. I go to prepare a place for you. And if I go and prepare a place for you, I will come again, and receive you to myself; that where I am, there you may be also" (John 14:2–3 NKJV). Since his ascension from the Mount of Olives about two thousand years ago, one of Jesus' primary concerns has been to prepare a heavenly home for his family. I like the word *mansion* simply because anything Jesus would create would be elegant. After all, he is the creator of all things; he has no problem getting supplies. The architect of the universe is preparing a home for you called the New Jerusalem. He cares that much about you.

As we look at a biblical view of heaven, bear in mind the words of the apostle Paul: "Eye has not seen, nor ear heard, nor have entered into the heart of man, the things which God has prepared for those who love him. But God has revealed them to us through his Spirit" (1 Cor. 2:9–10 NKJV). It is comforting to know that the Holy Spirit will at times reveal the mysteries of heaven in greater depth while we are still in this life. But even the writers of God's inspired Word could reveal only snapshots in comparison to the real thing. Heaven is far beyond what anyone can conceive or describe while on earth. The apostle John, who as an old man wrote the book of Revelation, also wrote the gospel that bears his name. He ended the gospel account of Jesus' ministry with an interesting verse: "Jesus did many other things as well. If every one of them were written down, I suppose that even the whole world would not have room for the books that would be written" (21:25). I can imagine that such an "I suppose" would be true of heaven as well.

Should you even try then to imagine what heaven would be like? Think about this. What if a couple were approaching marriage and the groom said, "Honey, we love each other so much, it doesn't make any difference where we live. I have a home for you in my heart. You don't need to know where we will be living." The bride might wonder about going through with the wedding. In his grace God gave us a written description of our home with him. Even though it is a limited picture, he knew it would help us on our journey.

In the Bible there are 151 references to heaven, speaking of the abode of God and of departed saints and the faithful angels; this is humankind's potential destiny. Ninety-seven of these references are in the New Testament, and fifty-four are in the Old Testament.[1] From Genesis to Revelation, heaven is addressed. Nearly two-thirds of the books of the Bible specifically mention heaven as the abode of God. Heaven, God's abode, is in the gospel accounts fifty-one times, and thirty-nine of those are Jesus' own words.

Heaven is a real place created by God. The Hebrew word for heaven is *shaymayim*. It refers both to a physical heaven and a spiritual realm of heaven. The root word is *shameh*, which means "lofty," referring more to the sky than to the abode of God. *Ouranos* in Greek means heaven as the "abode of God" or "happiness, power, eternity." It can also mean "elevation" or "sky."[2] In this book I am, of course, speaking of the abode of God. Scholars such as Robert Girdlestone see the words for heaven as dual in meaning, confirming a real place.[3]

In 2 Corinthians 12:2 Paul says that he was "caught up to the third heaven." In verse 4 he says he was "caught up to Paradise." As I said previously, this may have been a near-death experience. What does he mean by the "third heaven"? The Hebrews had a sense of there being three heavens. Two were natural heavens, one "near," where clouds form and birds fly, and a second one higher, where sun, moon, and stars exist. Then the third heaven, the home of God, was far beyond, the highest, farthest place.

Many Scriptures teach the concept that God is omnipresent, meaning the attribute of God by which he fills the universe and is present everywhere at once. "'Do not I fill heaven and earth?' declares the LORD" (Jer. 23:24). Yet from many other Scriptures, we know that a place called heaven is the habitation of God.

Do you remember how the Russian astronauts, near the beginning of human space exploration, reported with irony that they couldn't find heaven in outer space? Human beings find it hard to comprehend that God lives in a time-space dimension far beyond our experience. Hugh Ross, Ph.D. in astronomy, says the universe has at least eleven space-time dimensions proven by science since December 1994. Ross says, "The Bible is the only Holy Book that makes the claim that God is outside time. The Creator transcends the created."[4] God lives beyond the dimension that includes time effects. (I would add that perhaps his kingdom is beyond all dimensions.)

But what does heaven look like? If I prepared a travel brochure for you of my childhood home, Tampa, Florida, what I said would have to be in agreement with the Tampa Chamber of Commerce and the founders of that city. In preparing a travel brochure for you of heaven, I must share with you what Scripture, God's inspired Word to humans over the millennia, has to say.

This book is not intended to thoroughly deal with the issue of biblical authority, but archaeological digs continue to reveal the authenticity of the Scriptures. I became keenly aware of this in May 1996, when I went to Israel for the first time. On one of our tour days we visited the Shrine of the Book Museum in Jerusalem, the building whose roof is shaped like the jars in which the Dead Sea scrolls were found. There, stored behind protective glass, we

saw a two-thousand-year-old handwritten copy of the first chapter of
Isaiah in the original Hebrew language. This parchment of the entire
book of Isaiah was found in 1947, intact, wrapped in linen, covered
with black wax, and sealed in earthenware jars. W. F. Albright calls
it "the greatest manuscript discovery of modern times."[5]

Fragments of Ezekiel, including chapter 37, referring to
Israel's "dry bones" being restored, also dating back two thousand
years, have been found buried at Masada. This Scripture as well as
some from Deuteronomy and Psalms 81–85 "correspond almost
word for word with the present Hebrew Masoretic text."[6]

Grant Jeffrey notes, "The most incredible discovery was the
immense library of biblical manuscripts in Cave Four at Qumran
that contained every single book of the Old Testament with the
exception of the Book of Esther."[7] These are only a few of scores
of other finds confirming the endurance and accuracy of Scripture.

In preparation for my trip to Israel I pored over the "Pilgrim's
Map of the Holy Land" and "Visitor's Companion" tour information
brochure, watched video tapes of Israel, and saw a slide presentation by a friend who had visited there some years before. Then
I talked for hours on the phone with Pastor Randy Ticer and Polly
Perkins (a messianic Jew), both of whom had taken tour groups
to Israel many times. I wanted to be well prepared for my trip and
for guiding my group as its tour host.

Similarly, to write these chapters, I have studied the Scriptures. The Bible is the only reliable travel guide for such a journey.
While looking at the subject of heaven, I interpret the Bible in its
literal meaning unless the facts in the immediate context show
they should be interpreted otherwise. I have considered fundamental truths and looked at related passages of both Old and New
Testaments.

Many of the visual pictures of heaven are found in Revelation,
the last book of the Bible. Maybe you like angel stories. Here's one
where a messenger from God—an angel—brought the apostle
John great revelations of things past, present, and future. I'd say
that's an other-dimensional experience. God, being outside our
dimension, looked at the big picture and entrusted his revelation
to John, "the beloved" disciple. The last living apostle, John, was

exiled to Patmos, an island off the coast of Turkey, and there he received this vision. Some critics question the validity of Revelation or the relevance of its message for today. But seeming to be aware of man's doubts, the account opens with an admonishment: "Blessed is he who reads and those who hear the words of this prophecy, and keep those things which are written in it; for the time is near" (Rev. 1:3 NKJV).

Of John's writings in Revelation, Bible scholar Henry Halley says, "We believe absolutely that the book is exactly what it itself says it is; that it bears the stamp of its author; that some of its passages are among the most superb and most precious in all the Bible; that its climactic grandeur makes it a most fitting close to the Bible story; and that its glorious visions of the completed work of Christ make it a veritable roadway of God into the human soul."[8] He goes on to say that we should not be dogmatic in our opinions but keep a spirit of reverent humility and openness of mind as we seek to interpret Revelation. He sees it as a combination of historical and futuristic viewpoints. This is not a section to explain the complex but fascinating book of Revelation; rather, I intend to look at its descriptions of heaven as confirmed by the rest of the Bible.

In my discussion of heaven I focus my tour snapshots on several aspects that were evident in the NDEs noted in part 2. Keep in mind that, as with reading a tour guidebook or seeing a video or slides of Israel, we can visit only in part until we get there in person. I also focus on the major city of heaven, known as the New Jerusalem, so named in contrast to the Old Jerusalem on earth. This is one of the many descriptive names of heaven.[9] (Some others are Paradise, Father's house, a better country, City of the Living God, and so forth.) The Bible describes a future day when the New Jerusalem will descend to earth. Some of the following descriptions of heaven describe that "finished" city. Who knows, if Jesus went to prepare a place for us, maybe portions of the city are still under construction.

The Glorious Wall of the City

Remember Lorraine Tutmarc in chapter 8, and how she was fascinated with the first scene she viewed while walking toward the city of God? Transparent and shining, the wall extended as far as her eyes could see. Coming from behind it was music of perfect harmony from a heavenly choir accompanied by stringed instruments. She smelled the fragrance of flowers and she saw the compassionate face and penetrating eyes of Christ. Heaven includes a huge walled city, the New Jerusalem.

During my trip to Old Jerusalem I was deeply impressed as I observed the city's dramatic stone wall. It is eight to fourteen feet thick with what was a rampart, now a walkway, on top, wide enough for two people to walk shoulder to shoulder. The current wall was built by Sultan-Caliph Süleyman "between 1520 and 1566 on the same lines as the Roman fortifications" during Jesus' time. The ramparts are "between 39 to 49 feet high, and roughly 5,330 yards long, with eight gates; they give the city the shape of an irregular trapezium. In nearly five centuries, these fortifications have not changed significantly."[10] That wall, the Roman wall, and the wall around the city in David's day were all built to protect the city from its enemies.

The wall of heaven's New Jerusalem isn't there as protection from enemies, as we will have none. Along with other rebellious angels, Satan, at one time one of God's chief angels, was long ago cast out of heaven—for mutiny. So why is there a wall around the New Jerusalem? It is a constant reminder of our security in God. Isaiah describes it: "You will call your walls Salvation" (60:18). You will be surrounded by walls of salvation reminding you of the One who saved you from sin, selfishness, and spiritual death. In this fallen world I don't have to belabor the point that you and I live surrounded by gross sins and the awful results of them. The front page of most newspapers confirms this point.

What do the walls of the Holy City look like? In his revelation John wrote: "He [the angel] measured its wall and it was 144 cubits thick, by man's measurement, which the angel was using. The wall was made of jasper" (Rev. 21:17–18). Most scholars believe Scripture here is speaking of the width of the wall rather than the height. My reading indicated that this would be about 216 feet wide. (The Great Wall of China is only 20 feet wide.) We don't know how tall heaven's wall is, simply that it is tall, something compatible with the Pearl Gate (see discussion below). Verse 16 indicates that the city is a square, some 1,500 miles on each side. So the wall would be 6,000 miles long—nearly twice as long as the Great Wall of China (if you measured it in one piece). Elsewhere it is stated that the city is not a "simple" square but a cube, reminiscent of the Old Testament Holy of Holies, in which the glory of God was manifest on earth.

The size of the wall is itself mind-blowing, but the material it is made of is even more amazing. Jasper is a precious stone few of us are familiar with. Oriental Jasper is a sea-green quartz, its crystal perfectly clear. John says what he saw was a "precious jewel, like a jasper, clear as crystal" (Rev. 21:11). Transparent jasper would be the most valuable kind—flawless.

Some think that in antiquity jasper referred to a diamondlike stone. I like to think of it as a combination stone, because blue and green, the colors of sky and earth, are comforting to the eye, and diamondlike facets reflect the numerous aspects of our Messiah's beautiful character.

Revelation 21 continues: "The wall of the city had twelve foundations, and on them were the names of the twelve apostles. . . . The foundations of the city walls were decorated with every kind of precious stone" (vv. 14, 19). John then lists twelve stones, some familiar to us, some not so common: jasper, sapphire, chalcedony, emerald, sardonyx, sardius, chrysolite, beryl, topaz, chrysoprasus (chrysoberyl), jacinth (hyacinth), and amethyst.

Notice that if you compare this list of twelve gems to our beloved twelve-month list of birthstones you will find five of them to be the same: amethyst, February; emerald, May; sardonyx (peridot), August; sapphire, September; and topaz, November. A sixth birthstone is not listed as being in the wall but in the gate: the pearl, June. Next time you wear one of these birthstones, consider that you're wearing one of the same gems found in heaven's wall or gate. Yours is a small glimpse of what heaven will be like.

Viewing this sight, John must have been overwhelmed with the rainbow colors of the precious stones: transparent-sparkling blue-green, rich blue, lustrous blue-gray, bright green, orange-red, brilliant red, gold, sea green, lemon yellow with browns, yellow-green with bluish hue, deep red-brown, and luxurious purple. Heaven is certainly not a dull and lifeless place. Obviously God loves beauty.

John said that those twelve foundation stones had on them "the names of the twelve apostles of the Lamb" (21:14). Adam Clarke's picture is interesting: The city wall has twelve gates, and he proposes that the "twelve foundations" are thresholds to each gate. "On these were inscribed the names of the twelve apostles, to intimate that it was by the doctrine of the apostles that souls enter into the Church, and thence into the New Jerusalem."[11]

Take notice of how seriously God views the teachings of the apostles and how he honors them for eternity. Their foundational teachings, as laid out in our Apostles' and Nicene Creeds, and their witness help keep us steady on our journey of faith. That's a good reason to recite them often. Paul, speaking to the Ephesians, says, "Now, therefore, you are no longer strangers and foreigners, but fellow citizens with the saints and members of the household of God, having been built on the foundation of the apostles and prophets, Jesus Christ Himself being the chief cornerstone" (2:20 NKJV). Jesus is the initial foundation stone upon which our faith is built (1 Cor. 3:11).

The names of Jesus' twelve apostles deserve honorable mention here. Eight are sets of brothers. I've listed the brothers one after the other.

Simon Peter is listed first in all four biblical listings of the apostles. Upon meeting him, Jesus gave him a new surname, "'You are Simon son of John. You will be called Cephas' (which when translated, is Peter)" (John 1:42). His new name means "a rock." Peter was an outspoken, vacillating, enthusiastic disciple. After Jesus' resurrection Peter became a confident leader—the rock Jesus foresaw. Peter's sermon on Pentecost won three thousand souls to Christ.

Andrew was the first called of the twelve disciples (John 1:33–42). His greatest feat was leading his brother Peter to Christ with this proclamation: "We have found the Messiah" (John 1:41 NKJV).

James, son of Zebedee, has the distinction of being the first martyr of the Twelve. (Peter and James and his brother *John* were with Jesus at very intimate times, such as on the Mount of Transfiguration.)

John was honored by being called the beloved of Christ, which indicates his total devotion. He wrote the gospel that bears his name, three letters to the church, and the book of Revelation.

Philip is another disciple who brought his brother, *Bartholomew*, to Jesus, saying, "We have found him, of whom Moses in the law, and the prophets, did write, Jesus of Nazareth" (John 1:45 KJV). Philip was acquainted with the Scriptures. (He is not Philip, the deacon spoken of in Acts 6:5.)

Bartholomew was also called by a family name, Nathanael. To him Jesus gave an extraordinary compliment: "Behold an Israelite indeed, in whom there is no guile!" (John 1:47 KJV).

James the Less (Gk. *ho mikros*, "the little") was either of smaller stature or younger than the previously mentioned James, who is sometimes called "the Greater." The descriptions were simply to make it easier to distinguish between the two. *Judas surnamed Thaddaeus* (not Iscariot) was James's brother, both being sons of Alphaeus (Matt. 10:3; Luke 6:16).

The last four apostles are not believed to be brothers.

Simon Zelotes, as his name implies, was zealous for God, a fiery advocate of the Mosaic traditions and a student of the law.

Matthew, called Levi, was a tax collector until one day Jesus walked by his tax office and said, "Follow me."

Thomas was called Didymus, "the twin." Thomas doubted Jesus' resurrection until he saw him and touched his wounds. He then gave the best confession of faith in the entire gospel records: "My Lord and my God!" (John 20:28).

Matthias was chosen by "the eleven" to replace Judas Iscariot, who betrayed Jesus. While 120 followers waited for Pentecost in the Upper Room, Peter initiated the plan to choose another apostle—by sacred lot and prayer (Matt. 10:2–4; Acts 1:13, 15–26).

When you and I meet these men who gave all for the faith, it will be good to know their names and something about them. We will get more of the details on the other side of the heavenly wall.

Lorraine was drawn by the heavenly wall to want to go in. The brilliant biblical description of the wall can draw us to the wall of salvation. Isaiah prophesied, "In that day this song will be sung in the land of Judah: We have a strong city; God makes salvation its walls and ramparts" (26:1). In the heavenly New Jerusalem, the saints will look at the shining walls of jasper and burst forth in songs of praise for so great a salvation.

On my recent trip to Old Jerusalem I climbed stairs to the top of its wall as part of a prayer walk planned by the World Prayer Congress. To symbolize our prayer mission, hundreds of us put on white robes and walked around part of the city walls. What a beautiful sight—men and women in white walking, praying, or singing on the ramparts around the Old City. Occasionally a man would blow a ram's horn in praise. Others carried glorious banners. I saw "Prepare the Way of the Lord" in silver letters on royal blue and "Prince of Peace" in gold letters on shimmering blues and greens. It was a gift to be part of this committed group prayerfully claiming the city for God's purposes.

I can foresee being part of a similar march on heaven's walls—the saints worshiping, singing, dancing, and praising God. Think of the throng of people such a wide and beautiful sparkling jasper wall could handle!

Enter at the Gate of Pearl

You remember the NDE story of Deborah O'Donnell, who fell in her bathroom after working on the roof. She said, "As I was pulled out and up into the air, I saw that heaven was like a city. I could see a wall around it, and I could look into it, as if I were viewing it from an airplane. There was a gate at the entrance of this city. I wondered if this were the gate to the city of Jerusalem."

In his revelation John also saw the gates of New Jerusalem—gates made of pearls. "The twelve gates were twelve pearls, each gate made of a single pearl" (21:21). The pearl is a unique gem in that it does not come from the earth but from abnormal growth within an oyster. Pearls as big as city gates? Why not? One can look at the heavens and see how God creates things on a grand scale.

In a parable Jesus said, "The kingdom of heaven is like a merchant looking for fine pearls. When he found one of great value, he went away and sold everything he had and bought it" (Matt. 13:45–46). This truth has two parts. First, God is trying to impress us with the point that winning souls to God's kingdom is the supreme good that we should seek. The fine pearls are souls, and we should sacrifice our lives—that is, our time, talents, and finances—to obtain them for the kingdom. Proverbs says "He who wins souls is wise" (11:30).

Second, Jesus gave all he had for you. He came to find you, a pearl of great price. The great price was his life, the life of God incarnate. He gave it willingly out of total *agape* love. Jesus said, "No one takes it from Me, but I lay it down of Myself" (John 10:18 NKJV). He laid down his life for you.

When you come to the Pearl Gate to enter the city, you may find yourself on your knees in thanksgiving and praise for what Jesus Christ did for you—a precious pearl of great price. And maybe, when you get up, you will be filled with praise again as you look around and see some other glowing pearls who are there because of your life and witness.

Matthew Henry notes this about the gates and those who may enter: "As the city had four equal sides, answering to the four quarters of the world, so on each side there were three gates, signifying that there is as free an entrance from one part of the world as from the other."[11]

While writing this portion of the book, on September 8, 1996, my birthday, I woke up with a poem. Have you ever noticed how God likes to give you a gift on your birthday? Look for it the next time that special date comes around.

A Message from the Gates

If the Gates of Heaven could speak,
What would they say?

"Many come with pursed lips
Saying, "Oh, another day.
My life's so full and besides
There must be a different way."

Some say, "This gate's a pearl,
Too fine for me to enter.
I will seek another way
Plainer, broader, and deeper."

Others come to worship the gate
Who choose to stay outside.
They're quite comfortable there,
No commitment to come inside.

Some are here to take pictures
Of regal gates of solid pearl.
Want photos to show others
Saying, "I've been there, girls."

Others simply like to feel
My soft, luxurious outer coat.
Talk of the money I'd cost,
"Wouldn't that make folks dote?"

But what I like are those
Who use me for what I am.
Touch me gently, and then
Oh joy, they walk right in.

John says, "On the gates were written the names of the twelve tribes of Israel" (Rev. 7:4–8). Someone has well said that the Jewish faith is the bud and Christianity is the flower. We are reminded of this truth at the very gate of heaven. Jewish people pray to the God of Abraham, Isaac, and Jacob. The tribes of Israel come through this lineage, through the twelve sons of Jacob (also called Israel). Jesus was born into the tribe of Jacob's son Judah.

There is an Old Testament list that's somewhat different (Numbers 2). But here are the names of the tribes as listed in Revelation and their meanings:

Judah: confession or praise of God
Reuben: viewing the son
Gad: a company
Asher: blessed
Naphtali: wrestling with
Manasseh: forgetfulness
Simeon: hearing and obeying
Levi: cleaving to
Issachar: a reward

Zebulun: home

Joseph: added to

Benjamin: son of the right hand

As the twelve apostles' names on the foundations honor the saints of the New Testament, these names of the twelve tribes honor the faithful of the Old Testament.

Deborah O'Donnell had a message from God at the main gate of heaven. Does God have a coded message for you and me in these names on heaven's gates? I propose this meaning:

> Confessors and praisers of God, looking upon the Son, a band of, blessed ones, wrestling is over, forgetting the pain, hearing and obeying his Word, cleaving to our Lord, who is our reward, we are home, we are added to the family of Jesus, Son of the Father's right hand.

Note how the message begins with praise. And the Son is mentioned at the beginning and the end, so everything is tied to him. Through Scripture study over the years, I've often seen that the right hand of God refers to Jesus. Noting these clues, one can see a message at heaven's gate—for you, for all who will come.

If you study the twelve tribes you will note that Israel's first three sons—Reuben, Simeon, and Levi—get dishonorable mention in the Bible. Why should God now honor them by putting their names on the gates of heaven? They represent more than themselves; they represent their tribes. They remind us that physical Israel must become spiritual Israel—made up of Jews and Gentiles who acknowledge Jesus as the Messiah. All tribes and all who enter will be subject to Jesus Christ, who is the door and the only way into the city of God. "I am the way and the truth and the life. No one comes to the Father except through me," said Jesus (John 14:6). The names of these three men can remind us that we, too, have sinned, but through the atoning death of Jesus Christ we have been washed clean and made worthy to enter the gates.

With all this information from the Bible, what do you think the front door of heaven will be like? Perhaps the main Pearl Gate will have the tribe of Judah inscribed at the top and the apostle Peter's name on the foundation at the bottom. Or maybe all twelve of the apostles and tribes will be inscribed on all twelve of the gates.

Angels at the Gates

Perhaps you have been waiting for a snapshot of angels—the heavenly hosts. You will see them. In Luke 16:19–31 Jesus tells a parable about a beggar who died "and the angels carried him to Abraham's side," or bosom. Abraham's bosom was where the righteous waited until heaven's gates were opened at Jesus' triumphant entry into heaven after his death.

Craig Gottschalk met Jesus as Savior from spiritual death, and multitudes of angels rejoiced over him as his name was written in the Lamb's Book of Life. They rejoice at conversion, and how much more will they rejoice when you and I arrive at heaven's gate?

Heaven's angels are mighty spiritual beings who do God's bidding. In the New Testament the Greek word for angel (Gk. *angelos*) simply means "messenger." Angels are neither male nor female, have never sinned, and bear God's glory. Angels of God must not be worshiped, but when they speak one should pay attention. In chapter 6 Carolyn McCormick told her story of meeting an angel who helped her review her life, see God's omnipresence throughout every hurtful moment, and receive profound emotional healing for her soul.

In addition to bringing God's messages, they have other purposes: to love and praise God, to guard and protect believers, to encourage Christian obedience, to minister to those in spiritual battle, to receive departing saints, and to carry out God's justice.[13]

In his revelation of heaven John saw a guarding—not guardian—angel at each heavenly gate. The *Amplified Bible* describes the heavenly city: "It had a massive and high wall with twelve [large] gates, and at the gates [there were stationed] twelve angels" (Rev. 21:12). They are placed there for a purpose: to admit and receive the tribes of spiritual Israel (made up of Jews and Gentiles) and to rejoice when they see that we have made it. I think those of natural Israel who accept Jesus the Messiah will receive a special angelic "shalom" as they enter.

Jesus himself says, "Blessed are those who wash their robes, that they may have the right to the tree of life and may go through the gates into the city" (Rev. 22:14). White robes speak of the imputed righteousness we receive through Jesus; our own righteousness won't do here.

There is so much more that could be said about angels. If you want more information, read some of the books available—those with a biblical orientation being most accurate.

A Look Inside Heaven

You've now walked past the glorious walls and stepped through the most significant and beautiful gates imaginable. Once inside the walls "the street of the city [is] of pure gold, like transparent glass" (Rev. 21:21). Looking down you see that your feet are walking not on bricks or stones but on gold that is so pure it seems crystal clear. You are going to meet the King, and his building materials reflect his majesty. Some people have questioned the validity of gold's being transparent. But archaeologist Dr. Carl Baugh recently taught a series on television called *Understanding Creation.* Baugh learned from a NASA researcher, Danny Cook, that when gold is made thin enough it becomes transparent. Cook said that most metals in their purest state are transparent. "When our men walked on the moon, I did some of the research to make that possible. They wore visors and on their visors they had thin layers of transparent gold. The astronauts were able to look through the gold and it protected them from short-wave radiation."[14] If humans can make gold transparent, then God would have no trouble creating transparent gold, and as much as he wants.

In Old Jerusalem, during Christ's time on earth, the main street led from the Golden Gate on the east directly to the temple. In the New Jerusalem the main street of gold leads directly to the throne of God in the center of the city. Here is a throne, not a temple. John says, "I did not see a temple in the city, because the Lord God Almighty and the Lamb are its temple" (Rev. 21:22). The main street is unique to the others as there is a "river of the water of life, as clear as crystal, flowing from the throne of God and of the Lamb down the middle of the great street of the city. On each side of the river [stands] the tree of life, bearing twelve crops of fruit, yielding its fruit every month" (22:12).

Rebecca Springer, in her book *Within the Gates*, found that upon entering heaven she was to bathe in this river for healing. C. S. Lewis in his book *The Dawn Treader* envisions drinking the living water in heaven and finding that it satisfies as food does. (I discuss the Tree of Life below.)

And We Shall Behold Him

After you have been welcomed by the guarding angel and have walked through the amazing gate, your greatest experience will be seeing Jesus Christ. Remember how Deborah (chapter 4) delighted in thinking about the family members she loved, yet upon arrival the first thing she wanted to do was run to find Jesus, her Lord? What ecstasy it will be to be gathered into the arms of Jesus, the One who died for you and me. Since heaven is beyond earth's space-time dimension, it won't be any problem for Jesus to personally greet many arrivals just this intimately.

In Revelation, John gives several descriptions of Jesus. He is Ruler, Judge, and King. In a mind-boggling phrase John seems to use two paradoxical images: "For the Lamb ... will be their shepherd" (7:17).

About Jesus' nature Dr. Landry says, "Then Jesus glanced at me with a look of compassion, full of love and caring. A glance similar, I imagine, to the look he gave his mother, Mary, and his friend John as they waited in agony at the foot of the cross. This glance was the essence of love. *I understood the fullness of the love of God at that moment.*" Lorraine Tutmarc says about him, "He looked down at me. He had such beautiful eyes. I'll never forget those eyes. They were so large and full of meaning—and kindness and forgiveness and compassion. *Everything you would want to see in Jesus' face was there.*" When Jesus looks into your eyes you'll never be the same. You'll experience transformation, rapture, ecstasy.

Jesus will want to take you to the Father. After Jesus' resurrection and before his ascension, he spoke powerful words to Mary Magdalene (I think with a big smile on his face): "Go to My brethren and say to them, 'I am ascending to My Father and your Father, and to My God and your God'" (John 20:17 NKJV). He came to earth to save us from destruction and to bring us into his family. He longed for his Father to become our Father and was ecstatic that his work had been completed. The greatest description

Jesus gives of his Father is that of an earthly father eagerly waiting for his wayward child to come home and running out to meet him (Luke 15:11–32). When we finally reach home, our Father will comfort us and tell us that he loves us with the same love with which he loves his firstborn Son (John 17:26).

The Throne of God

When John looked at the scene in heaven, his focal point of attention was the throne of God. He said, "Behold, a throne set in heaven, and One sat on the throne" (Rev. 4:2 NKJV). A throne is the seat in which a king sits on ceremonial occasions. Valvita Jones saw God's throne as being transparent and extending from heaven to earth, which reflects the Scripture,

> *Thus says the LORD: "Heaven is My throne,*
> *And earth is My footstool.*
> *Where is the house that you will build Me?*
> *And where is the place of my rest?"*
>
> (Isa. 66:1 NKJV; cf. Matt. 5:35)

You've seen thrones on television. Queen Elizabeth's throne in the House of Lords, at the Palace of Westminster is the most familiar. At the annual State Opening of Parliament, the queen processes to her throne wearing the crown jewels and the crimson robe of state with its eighteen-foot train carried by no fewer than four pages of honor.

The Old Testament portrays Solomon's throne as the most magnificent in the world at that time (1 Kings 10:20). It was made of ivory and plated with gold; the back was round, and it had two arm supports. On the ascent of six steps stood twelve lions made of gold.

But God's throne outshines all earthly thrones. Streets of gold lead up to the throne. Isaiah describes a heavenly vision: "I saw the Lord seated on a throne, high and exalted, and the train of his robe filled the temple" (6:1). God's power is greater than all thrones that have ever existed, for all ages added together. His throne extends from the center of heaven to the center of earth and into the universe.

Revelation 4 lays out a description of the heavenly throne. This description precedes an account of the throne-room scene when the seals are broken and judgment begins on the earth, on Satan, his fallen angels, and others who have turned their backs on God's grace. Here Jesus, through his self-sacrificial love, has conquered the power of evil that plagued the earth since its beginning. This is the reason for all the rejoicing in this account. Some parts of this may be descriptive of a particular event, but let's see what John saw at the throne of God.

> And He who was sitting was like a jasper stone and a sardius in appearance; and there was a rainbow around the throne, like an emerald in appearance.... And from the throne proceed flashes of lightning and sounds and peals of thunder. And there were seven lamps of fire burning before the throne, which are the seven Spirits [sevenfold Spirit] of God; and before the throne there was, as it were, a sea of glass like crystal. (4:3, 5–6 NASB)

God is the glory here, shining as diamondlike jasper mixed with the fiery red sardius stone. The fiery red of his countenance probably speaks of the judgment about to fall on earth. The emeraldlike rainbow around the throne reminds of God's promise in Genesis never to destroy the world again by flood; it helps us know that he is a faithful promise keeper. The circle speaks of eternity in heaven, which is his gift to those who receive his Son. The lamps of fire are more like torches lit before battle and represent the refining fire and work of the Holy Spirit.

The sea of glass like crystal is the floor of the throne room. Moses also had a vision of heaven just before he was given the Ten Commandments: "Moses ... saw the God of Israel. Under his feet was something like a pavement made of sapphire, clear as the sky itself " (Ex. 24:9–10). The foundation is like a crystal sea of blue sapphire—awesome, glorious, breathtaking.

And around the throne are flashes of color and brilliant light. It reminds me of the times I visited the winter wonderland of Alaska. Several times I saw the awe-inspiring Northern Lights with their iridescent colors flashing across the sky. There's even a little humming noise that goes with it. I think the throne will be something like that.

The majesty of the Revelation 4 throne scene continues. We see twenty-four thrones around God's throne. "Surrounding the throne were twenty-four other thrones, and seated on them were twenty-four elders. They were dressed in white and had crowns of gold on their heads . . . the twenty-four elders fall down before him who sits on the throne, and worship him who lives for ever and ever" (Rev. 4:4, 10).

As you might guess, these elders are the twelve tribes of Israel and the twelve apostles. They also represent believers who will judge the world (Rev. 20:4; cf. 1 Cor. 6:2–3), wearing white robes, the garments of the faithful in heaven, and golden crowns, rewards for the faithful. You too will fall down when you behold our glorious Father God.

The cherubim add further glory to the throne scene as they guard the holiness of God. In the creation story cherubim protected the entrance to the Garden of Eden; here they guard the throne of God.

> In the center, around the throne, were four living creatures, and they were covered with eyes, in front and in back. The first living creature was like a lion, the second was like an ox, the third had a face like a man, the fourth was like a flying eagle. Each of the four living creatures had six wings and was covered with eyes all around, even under his wings. Day and night they never stop saying:

> *"Holy, holy, holy*
> *is the Lord God Almighty,*
> *who was, and is, and is to come."*
>   (Rev. 4:6–8)

This description reveals the nature of cherubim. They are brave as a lion, they serve like an ox, they are insightfully wise as humankind, and they are swift like an eagle to carry out God's purposes. Dr. Landry said that in heaven he was able simultaneously to see in front of and behind himself. Even more so, that seems to be the case with these angels. They offer constant praise to God and proclaim his holiness.

The book of Hebrews indicates that Jesus—at least at specific times—is right there in the throne room. "Jesus . . . sat down at the right hand of the throne of God" (Heb. 12:2; see also 8:1). In Revelation 5 he is depicted as the Lamb of God. And tens of thousands of angels are singing:

> *"Worthy is the Lamb, who was slain,*
> *to receive power and wealth and wisdom and strength*
> *and honor and glory and praise!" (v. 12)*

And then "every creature" joins in singing:

> *"To him who sits on the throne and to the Lamb*
> *be praise and honor and glory and power,*
> >   *for ever and ever!"*

> The four living creatures said, "Amen," and the elders fell down and worshiped. (vv. 13–14)

Through the writer of Hebrews, God tells believers still walking this earth how to come to his throne. "Let us therefore come boldly to the throne of grace, that we may obtain mercy, and find grace to help in time of need" (4:16 NKJV). Every time you pray you are coming to God's awesome throne. To his children it is the throne of grace, of God's unmerited favor.

If you arrive in heaven before the day of God's grace has ended on earth, the throne scene may not be quite as overwhelming as the one described in Revelation 4. There, judgment of evil on the earth is about to begin

Your Arrival

I've tried to give you a picture of part of heaven. Walk through what I imagine the scene might be like upon your arrival—or mine—at the gates of the New Jerusalem.

Happily step through the gates noticing every detail, the names on the gate, even the welcoming wink from the angel guarding the gate. You're urged to come right in. The wide walls make for a long corridor; the jasper glistens and reminds you of a rainbow effect of lights.

Walking is so easy, "more like flowing" than walking. At the entrance you stand awestruck, feeling perfect peace and seeing awesome beauty. Leading to God's throne, I imagine you'll see a green parklike boulevard running up both sides of the inviting river. On the boulevard grow Trees of Life laden with mouthwatering fruit of many colors. In Genesis this fruit was known to cause one to live forever. Now you'll at last be permitted to eat it since you're no longer in a sinful, fallen condition. On each side of the boulevards are the main streets of gold leading into the city. You're actually seeing the heavenly streets you've only heard or read about. Yes, it is all true. You wonder what to do first.

Perhaps you'll choose to take a swim in the River of Life, then walk along the golden boulevard. An angel may hand you a piece of fruit from the Tree of Life to refresh you from your journey. You'll savor every bite.

Then like a compass your thoughts will turn to finding Jesus and *Abba*, Father. (Hebrew and Aramaic children call their fathers "Abba," which, like "Papa," denotes affection and tenderness.) Jesus called his Father "Abba" (Mark 14:36) and now, through him, you have that privilege too.

A good place to find Jesus is at his Father's right hand. What a glorious throne Jesus must have. I think he will come down the glorious steps to meet you because he has been longing for this day of welcome.

Gerard Landry was greeted with Jesus' peace. Perhaps our Lord will say to you, "My sister (or my brother), my betrothed, shalom, and welcome home." When he takes you in his arms to embrace you, his peace permeates even further into your entire being. You'll want to see his nail-pierced hands, hold them tenderly, and perhaps kiss them, as you thank him for dying for you. The fragrance of his anointing reminds you of roses and lilies. Or is it myrrh and frankincense? As you look into his eyes, such joy fills you that it is like all the birthdays and all the Christmases you've ever had rolled into one. You laugh together. Never have you felt loved more than this here in his immediate presence. You're completely fulfilled and satisfied. Every pain you've ever suffered has melted away.

You talk a while, and he tells you about the home he has prepared for you. Remembering this heavenly Carpenter was in that trade on earth, you are eager to see his creation. All of a sudden you see an angel standing nearby. You're introduced to your childhood guardian angel who is eager to show you around. You embrace Jesus but you know there will never be any more real good-byes. You and your angel host have catching up to do with earth talk—finding out how he helped you out of many dangerous jams. You're full of excitement while heading for your home to see your family and friends.

After all this, Jesus will present you to Abba, Father who has watched over your life from its beginning. You had often prayed, "Our Father who art in heaven," and now you are actually with your Father *and* in heaven. He has longed for you to be a member of his family. Abba will show you what a real Father's love is like. He will give you a loving hug just as the father did with the prodigal son. You can tell he is pleased with you. All this in the presence of the comforting Holy Spirit. The events go from "glory to glory," as Scripture so aptly describes.

Family members and friends will have learned about your arrival and will be there at your new residence to greet you and rejoice. Yes, you'll know your loved ones in heaven. Perhaps even your favorite animal will be there.

Until the future day of resurrection, you and your loved ones will have spirit bodies that have form but can be seen through. Dr. Landry noted this when he said, "When you look at yourself and can look through yourself, it is quite an experience."

The apostle Paul, who had a "to heaven and back" experience, said, "For now we see in a mirror, dimly, but then face to face. Now I know in part, but then I shall know just as I also am known" (1 Cor. 13:12 NKJV). This may be speaking of spiritual and physical "knowing." And this is a great comfort. I will know my husband, my mother, and my father just as they were known to me on earth. I will not see my mother after ten reincarnations and have to be reintroduced to her. Reincarnation is not a reality, and it negates the value of Jesus' death for humankind. "Man is destined to die once," says Hebrews 9:27. Your present life is not a dress rehearsal. It is your one and only life.

Some of us may arrive in heaven not through natural death but on the day when "the Lord Himself will descend from heaven with a shout, with the voice of an archangel, and with the trumpet of God. And the dead in Christ will rise first. Then we who are alive and remain shall be caught up together with them in the clouds to meet the Lord in the air. And thus we shall always be with the Lord" (1 Thess. 4:16–17 NKJV). Not everyone will hear this trumpet blast. Only those who love Christ's appearing will hear the call, so keep your ears tuned heavenward. Those who enter heaven on this day will meet deceased loved ones who are now reunited with their resurrected, glorified bodies. Your own earthly body will have been transformed into a glorified, incorruptible body as fast as the blink of an eye (1 Cor. 15:52). (More of this in chapter 13.)

How do I envision the environment of heaven? Once you've arrived, you've only just begun to live. The adventure has started. You are totally safe for the first time. There is nothing to be afraid of. No evil spirits are around to tempt you. You have no pain physically or emotionally. All you feel is love, peace, and security surrounding you. No experience on earth can compare to the ecstasy you feel just being in the presence of God, worshiping him, delighting in the music you hear and help create. Light is everywhere because Jesus' omnipresent glory is the light of the city. "The city does not need the sun or the moon to shine on it, for the glory of God gives it light, and the Lamb is its lamp" (Rev. 21:23).

Remember what Valvita Jones said about Jesus' light? "There now seemed to be a heavenly illumination that caused his hair to be light red and his eyes bluish, almost transparent, and his skin a light golden color. There is no way to fully describe his coloring. It is like another world's color. It's the Shechinah glory, iridescent golden light glowing through him. In his resurrection body, his coloring is uniquely different from anything on earth." Pam Johnstone describes it: "I saw someone ahead of me. . . . The light was shining behind the person, maybe coming from the garments. I kept walking, trying to make out who the person was." And Lorraine Tutmarc says, "All the darkness was gone out of my life, gone completely! A brilliance, but it wasn't sunshine, came from Jesus. A transparent gold light came from him, from his body."

In heaven our physical senses—smell, taste, hearing, sight—are heightened beyond our earthly imagination. One young woman who talked to me about her near-death experience said that she had a most wonderful picnic in the park with friends and family. The flowers surrounding them were beyond anything she had seen on earth and their fragrance was literally out of this world. Remember how Lorraine Tutmarc smelled the sweet fragrance of flowers and heard birds singing? I imagine heavenly gardens that bespeak refreshment, as if Eden were transplanted in heaven and then reproduced in many different locations.

I look forward to Scripture classes with Jesus, where he will explain every question you and I ever had biblically and personally. That in itself will take quite a bit of time, or should I say untime, with all the interests of heaven's inhabitants being addressed. Maybe he will let some of the well-versed saints teach basics to those who have never learned much from his Word. We'll have a lot to learn as we prepare ourselves for the high calling of ruling and reigning with Christ.

Ruling and reigning? Yes. There will be work for you to do. At the appointed time you will be given orders on how God wants you to assist him in the battle to put down evil and to restore and heal the world. God's army of saints and angels will come back with Jesus to stop the bloodshed at Armageddon, defeat Satan's army, and put them in *Gehenna* where they can do no more harm.

We will assist our Messiah in his thousand-year reign on earth. I imagine many teams helping to clean up the earth's pollution—in the time of the restoration of all things (Acts 3:21).

And then the city of New Jerusalem will come down from heaven as a bride beautifully dressed for her husband.

Don't Miss the Party

I'm looking forward to the wedding and getting to dance with my Bridegroom on the streets of gold. Several years ago when I visited musicians Jim and Sheila Todd in Virginia, they played on keyboard and violin a song about dancing on the streets of gold. Our gathered group was rejoicing and singing when I had a sweet inner picture of myself dancing with Jesus on heaven's streets. As I saw it, gold made a good dance floor. I was enjoying myself, absorbed in his love. It was wonderful.

Then after a while someone tapped on Jesus' shoulder. It was Dennis cutting in. How thrilling it was to dance with Dennis again. Of course, both of us danced much better in heaven than on earth (and we had enjoyed dancing together on special occasions and sometimes around the kitchen and living room).

After a while, someone else tapped on Dennis's shoulder. It was my dad. How fun it was to dance with Dad, who on earth never believed a Christian should dance. He was quite a good dancer too. I found out how much fun he could be.

Then, to my surprise, someone tapped on Dad's shoulder. It was Jesus again. We danced and danced and, since there is no time there, I don't know how long it was, but it was true ecstasy. I saw this creative scene, though not a vision, as a little foretaste of heaven.

All over heaven you and multitudes of others can be dancing on transparent gold streets to the music of angels' harps, violins, flutes, and trumpets. The New Jerusalem is filled with and surrounded by music. Hundreds of thousands may be dancing on heaven's jasper walls. Old and New Testament saints you have always wanted to meet will be there, too, plus thousands from more recent history. And, yes, beloved family members and friends will be there. Everyone will be rejoicing together.

God is throwing a party in heaven. Everybody has been invited, but some have chosen not to come. Others have been too busy to respond. If you haven't done so already, I hope you'll be wise enough to RSVP to your invitation immediately.

CHAPTER ELEVEN

Rewards for the Greatest Olympic Game

Well done, good and faithful servant! You have been faith-
ful with a few things; I will put you in charge of many
things. Come and share your master's happiness!

Jesus, King of Kings
Matthew 25:21

———◆———

What if you were born to be a king and you lived and died
without ever finding out? That would be a pretty sad situation. I
want to break the news to you: You are called to be a king—one
day to rule and reign with Christ. In heaven kings are both male
and female. Gender in heaven is not as specific as on earth. Brides,
sons, kings—these are designations that apply to all God's children. As a child of God—as the bride of Christ—kingship is your
destiny.

Kings wear crowns. The two simply go together. In heaven
it's possible that all who run the race to the end will receive a
crown for that event alone. But there are other crowns—gold
ones—that God will give for special achievements, which we will
look at shortly.

As the twenty-four elders cast their golden crowns before
God's throne, so you will first of all offer your crown back to God,
placing it at the foot of Jesus' throne (see Rev. 2:10; 3:11). Then
possibly he will place it back on your head—Scripture doesn't

say—maybe you will get it back so that you can lay it at his feet again from time to time as an act of love and submission.

The crowns could be strictly spiritual, but if that is the case, I wonder why the apostle John wrote that he saw them on the elders' heads. Note also that Dr. Landry (chapter 5) saw the saints with crowns in their hands. Just as our bodies will be of a different substance than when on earth, I imagine that our heavenly crowns will have otherworldly qualities but be no less real than a crown worn by an earthly king or queen.

The fourth verse of *Love Divine*, a well-loved hymn by Charles Wesley, says:

> *Finish then thy new creation, pure and spotless let us be;*
> *Let us see thy great salvation perfectly restored in thee:*
> *Changed from glory into glory, till in heaven we take*
>   *our place,*
> *Till we cast our crowns before thee, lost in wonder,*
>   *love, and praise!*

Author Grant Jeffrey notes: "It is my conviction, after hundreds of discussions with Christians, that one of the great reasons for the lack of holiness in the Church today is that we have lost sight of the rewards of Heaven."[1] Perhaps the trend will change. I see a need for a balance between the subjects of rewards and grace. We know all accolades are by God's grace alone, yet ignoring the subject of rewards seems a mistake.

Grace and Works

When my husband, Dennis, would thank his congregation for a project well done, he would try to remember everyone who had participated. But sometimes a name would slip from his memory or not get on the list. Knowing this was always a possibility, he would end by saying, "For those of you whose names have been accidentally omitted, I want you to know that you'll get your reward in heaven." You could see the wheels turning, *Oh, I wish my good deed would have gotten credited to the other side.* I expect most of us would like the best of both worlds—credit here and reward later.

In his writings Paul lays out a balanced approach to works and grace. The well-known meaning of grace is "God's unmerited favor." An acrostic I've heard for grace is "**G**od's **R**iches **A**t Christ's **E**xpense. This expense is beyond all others—the death of God's only Son to rescue you and me.

At one point in my life I especially needed a grace (nonlegalistic) church to draw me closer to God. The basic message I received in my senior year at the university Episcopal chapel was *yes, I'm unworthy, no doubt about it, but God loves me anyway, and by Jesus' death I'm made worthy to stand before God*. This was the beginning of my deeper commitment to Christ. Now whenever I need a good dose of grace, I can find it at my church exquisitely presented by my pastor, Dorsey McConnell. No one who has listened to one-quarter of the sermon leaves the church feeling self-righteous. As Dorsey says, "The way you get before God is to admit you don't deserve to stand there. You pray, 'Lord Jesus Christ, have mercy on me a sinner.'" He says that when we build on the foundation stone of Christ, the first building block is a spirit of repentance, the second is the spirit of love, and third is giving that love away to others.

I was christened in infancy as a Presbyterian, raised and baptized in the Assemblies of God, was a Southern Baptist in my teens, was confirmed as a young adult and continue to the present as an Episcopalian, and now am also at times enjoying fellowship in Messianic Christian churches. I love all denominations, as I believe each has a particular treasure to share. But rest assured, there won't be any denominations in heaven. People joke about how heaven is divided up into different parts for each denomination, but that idea is just that—a joke.

Denominations are only earthly distinctions. In heaven you may reminisce about your group with some of your friends, but if you tell an angel you're of a certain denomination, don't be surprised if he looks at you blankly. Here and now is the time for that, not in heaven.

I trust that your group has or will lead you to Christ, but being a card-carrying "whatever" won't get you or me through the heavenly gate. In heaven two appropriate theme songs will be "Amazing Grace" and one that begins "We Are One in the Spirit." While on earth, enjoy your church, messianic fellowship, or synagogue. Give it all you've got. Worship brings you a bit of heaven on earth. The hymns and worship songs are such contrast to the world, that just stepping in the doors gives one an "otherworld" atmosphere.

Keeping the balance of works and grace in mind—we are saved by grace, we are by grace rewarded for our works—let's go on and talk about God's rewards to the faithful, to those united as one forever.

The Olympics

The 1996 Olympic Games in Atlanta made for quite a sensation. It is estimated that 60 percent of the world's population watched them. Most of us don't realize that the Olympic games began in Athens, Greece, before the time of Christ, 776 B.C. The games were celebrated every four years, which was termed an *Olympiad*. The apostle Paul's epistles abound with allusions to the Greek contests, so he may well have attended the Olympics, gleaning imagery from the games.

Speaking of Paul's sport-related images and the early Greek Olympic games, Adam Clarke says, "It is sufficiently evident that the apostle alludes to the athletic exercises in the games which were celebrated every [fourth] year on the isthmus, or narrow neck of land, which joins the Peloponnesus, or Morea, to the main land; and were therefore termed the Isthmian games. These exercises were running, wrestling, boxing, throwing the discus or quoit, [etc.]; to the three first of these the apostle especially alludes."[2]

Three kinds of races in the original Olympics are clearly shown in *Unger's Bible Dictionary*. "First, a simple match in the stadium (1 Cor. 9:24–27), the race being run in heats of four, the first in the final heat being proclaimed victor; later the runners had to make a circuit of the goal and return to the starting point; then came the long race, where the distance of the stadium had to be covered six, seven, eight, twelve, twenty, or twenty-nine times."[3] This long-distance race, or perhaps all these races together, describe our earthly race most clearly.

Note some of Paul's "running the race" statements:

> I press toward the mark for the prize of the high calling
> of God in Christ. (Phil. 3:14 KJV)
>
> Do you not know that those who run in a race all run,
> but one receives the prize? Run in such a way that you may
> obtain it. And everyone who competes for the prize is tem-
> perate in all things. Now they do it to obtain a perishable
> crown, but we for an imperishable crown. Therefore I run
> thus: not with uncertainty. Thus I fight: not as one who beats
> the air. But I discipline my body and bring it into subjection,
> lest, when I have preached to others, I myself should become
> disqualified. (1 Cor. 9:24–27 NKJV)

"Disqualified" doesn't mean that you get kicked off the team,
but that you miss the special awards God has waiting for you. You
don't need great athletic skills to get in the race; everyone who
accepts Jesus Christ gets in.

Paul says that the best way to run a race is to keep focused
on the goal ahead. You must keep right on to the end of the race.
Being sloppy isn't going to cut it. The Rev. Dick Mills says, "Getting
from this world to the next is compared to a foot race. Life is not
a hundred-yard dash to glory. It is more like a long-distance
marathon."[4] Track meets and marathons are sports in which com-
petitors are rewarded individually for how well they do.

This race of living our lives to glorify Christ is different from
the ones run in the Atlanta Olympics or in a school meet, because
here we are not striving to beat out the other runners. Rather, our
motivation is to do the best for God's sake. In a spiritual race each
one can win. Then some in their faithfulness go on to receive special awards. Mills explains:

> According to the terminology used by Paul in 1 Corin-
> thians 9:24, there is only one winner. The one who comes in
> first gets the award. In the modern-day Olympics there are
> three winners: gold, silver, and bronze medalists.[5]

Using another sports analogy, Paul mentions the boxer not
accomplishing anything if he is just beating the air rather than
delivering a good punch. To participate in any sporting event one

needs to keep one's body in good shape. It is amazing to hear how very young many contestants are when they begin to train for the Olympics. I know one Olympic athlete, figure skater Janet Lynn (now Solomon). Like most young Olympic contenders she undoubtedly had little or no time to play after school because extracurricular life was spent in *practice*. Olympic athletes and their parents give up much to aim for the highest. The victory is obviously worth it to them. In comparison, how many of us are so serious about God's events that we work hard at keeping our spiritual lives in shape?

In the early Greek games, winners received crowns made of greenery, which of course eventually faded away.

> The crown won by the victor in the Olympian games was made of the wild olive; in the Pythian games of laurel; in the Nemean games of parsley; and in the Isthmian games of the pine. These were all corruptible, for they began to wither as soon as they were separated from the trees, or plucked from the earth. In opposition to these, the apostle says, he contended for an incorruptible crown, the heavenly inheritance. He sought not worldly honour; but that honour which comes from God.[6]

Along with Paul, you may well have awaiting you crowns far greater than a victor's garland of wild olive, laurel, parsley, or pine, greater even than a medal of bronze, silver, or gold—as wonderful as those are. Let's see what kind of everlasting crowns God is offering you and me.

Watcher's Crown (or Crown of Righteousness)

I have chosen to list first the watcher's crown, given to all those who look for the return of Christ. Paul says, "Finally, there is laid up for me the crown of righteousness, which the Lord, the righteous Judge, will give to me on that Day, and not to me only but also to all who have loved His appearing" (2 Tim. 4:8 NKJV).

Do you think about Jesus' return when you go to bed at night, wake up in the morning, or go about your day? Do you think, *Maybe today is the day my Lord will come?* Or, *I wish Jesus would come and start his reign soon and straighten out this mess we're in?* Do you study God's Word to see what it says about Jesus' coming? If so, you are an active watcher. If you're dreading the idea with thoughts of, "Oh I'm so unworthy; I hope he doesn't come today," then I suggest you seek biblical counsel and healing prayer. Yes, we are all unworthy—that's why Jesus died. But no believer should dread the day of the Lord's coming.

Looking for Jesus' return has a way of purifying the soul. The apostle John says, "Beloved, now we are children of God; and it has not yet been revealed what we shall be, but we know that when He is revealed, we shall be like Him, for we shall see Him as He is. And everyone who has this hope in Him purifies himself, just as He is pure" (1 John 3:2–3 NKJV). John quotes the Lord as saying, "Behold, I am coming as a thief. Blessed is he who watches, and keeps his garments, lest he walk naked" (Rev. 16:15 NKJV). Your daily watch is drawing you closer to Christ. If you are a Watcher you're in good company, because angels are called "watchers" and "holy ones" (Dan. 4:13, 17 NKJV).

I have noticed that losing a very dear person in death often prompts a believer to become a more intent watcher. And watching does a deep work in a person's life. This daily activity can create a more righteous lifestyle. By righteous I don't mean prudish, or self-righteous; I refer, rather, to right thinking, acting, and speaking. One becomes more like Jesus. As I noted in chapter 2, one's mind is set on things above.

Soul Winner's Crown (or Crown of Rejoicing)

The second crown we'll look at is the soul winner's crown.

"For what is our hope, or joy, or crown of rejoicing? Is it not even you in the presence of our Lord Jesus Christ at His coming? For you are our glory and joy" (1 Thess. 2:19–20 NKJV).

Here the apostle Paul was writing to the suffering Christians of Thessalonica in Macedonia. Paul was so brutally persecuted that he couldn't travel to Thessalonica to watch over his converts. He expressed love and longing for them much like a father for his children. The *Living Bible* gives this paraphrase of the passage: "For what is it we live for, that gives us hope and joy and is our proud reward and crown? It is you! Yes, you will bring us much joy as we stand together before our Lord Jesus Christ when he comes back again. For you are our trophy and joy" (vv. 19–20). Paul lived for his spiritual children. They gave him hope and joy and were his reward and crown. When he stands with them at Christ's return, they will be spiritual trophies he can give to the Lord. Paul's joy in living was helping others find true salvation for every part of their being—body, soul, and spirit.

Daniel 12:3 notes that on the future Day of the Lord, "Those who are wise will shine like the brightness of the heavens, and those who lead many to righteousness, like the stars for ever and ever." Not only will these witnesses have golden crowns, but they will also shine as bright luminaries. I can easily pick the planet Venus out in the sky at night because it shines so brightly. Similarly soul winners will have a lot of "shine" to their countenance.

One great way to be a soul winner is by your life. You don't know who is looking at you and watching to see if your actions line up with your words. This life witness may be a long process—someone may size you and your Christian walk up for a long time before making a decision to turn to Christ—but it can be powerful and "winning."

Some of us may witness for Christ without consciously intending to do so. For example, before I walked in the power of the Holy Spirit, I was a "closet Christian." If some part of my life did not contribute to making me popular, I'd keep quiet about it. This meant that I kept quiet about my faith. But in 1955 as a contestant in a beauty contest, I was asked who I most wanted to be like. I was absolutely shocked at my answer: "There's no one on earth I want to be like, but One in heaven, and that is Jesus Christ." Years later, looking back on this experience, I understood the difference between my born-again spirit (Gk. *pneuma*), which was willing, and my born-again soul (Gk. *psyche*), which was still partially carnal and compromising. One teenager came up to me afterward and said, "You answered the questions best of all." Maybe I reached one life, but I can take absolutely no credit, because it just "happened."

In time I became better prepared to witness effectively. I received training at a Billy Graham crusade in 1963. And that, coupled with a previous anointing of the Spirit, gave me a new enthusiasm, confidence, and power. (Peter was an unwilling witness until after the Day of Pentecost, when in that one day he won three thousand souls.) Although bringing people into the kingdom is exciting, we personally can take little credit, for the Holy Spirit is the real soul-winner.

Evangelism ranks high in the priorities of ourKing (Matt. 28:19). I hope you, too, will "go for" this crown as you continue on your journey. Your life will be one of rejoicing—along with the angels in heaven who rejoice when a lost soul is brought into the Shepherd's fold (Luke 15:10).

Crown of Purity (or Incorruptible Crown)

"Do you not know that those who run in a race all run, but one receives the prize? Run in such a way that you may obtain it. And everyone who competes for the prize is temperate in all things. Now they do it to obtain a perishable crown, but we for an imperishable [or incorruptible] crown. Therefore I run thus: not with uncertainty" (1 Cor. 9:24–26 NKJV). For this crown the key word is *temperate*—which refers to a life marked by moderation, not having extreme or excessive appetites or desires. It is characteristic of a life of purity. *Webster's New Collegiate Dictionary* defines *pure* as "free from what weakens, or pollutes, free from moral fault or guilt." Freedom from weakness, inner pollution, and guilt probably sounds good to you. It does to me—though it doesn't sound much like the world we live in.

Does God want us to live pure, temperate lives because he wants to take our fun away? Of course not. He wants us to be happy and fulfilled in every way. The safety rules he gave us are for our joy to be increased, not diminished. Relate this to a good football, basketball, or golf game and you'll see what I mean. A game with no rules would be no fun, no game at all. If there had been no rules to the contests at the recent Olympic games, millions of people wouldn't have spent days glued to their TV screens.

God has given us game rules that work so everyone can be happy to the fullest. But that doesn't mean there isn't effort involved.

Adam Clarke quotes an ancient description of what Olympic athletes experienced.

> *Temperate in all things.* All those who contended in these exercises went through a long state and series of painful preparations. Epictetus asks, "Do you wish to gain the prize at the Olympic games? Consider the requisite preparations and the consequences: you must exercise yourself at the necessary and prescribed times both in heat and in cold; you must drink nothing cooling . . . in a word, you must put yourself under the directions of a pugilist, as you would under those of a physician, and afterwards enter the lists. Here you may get your arm broken, your foot put out of joint, be obliged to swallow mouthfuls of dust, to receive many stripes, and after all be conquered."[7]

It takes endurance, discipline, and commitment to be an Olympian. Should we as followers of Jesus be careless in our life's witness for him before the world and powers of darkness? We can't be perfect—Romans 3:10 says, "There is no one righteous, not even one"—but if we fall down, we can pick ourselves up, wash off, and get back into the race. The important things are to stay in, not give up, and improve our race. Let's do our best for Christ, become Olympians for his sake.

When we accepted Jesus he gave us his righteousness, a new nature, and a desire to live right. And yet none of us goes through life without the need to confess daily sins in thought, word, or deed—"not even one." Confession is a daily discipline we can do, for example, by praying the Lord's Prayer (Matt. 6:9–13). Before entering the heavenly gates, we will need to repent of our every sin, allowing Christ to cleanse our souls.

Heaven will be full of cleansed sinners wearing incorruptible crowns. I expect to see Mary Magdalene, who, though once demon-possessed due, in part, to her life of sexual compromise, was set free by Jesus. And King David, who took another man's wife and had her husband killed but fully repented. And Craig Gottschalk, who turned from the drug culture and gave his life to God. And you and I, who have repented and received Jesus, will be there to receive an incorruptible crown. It doesn't matter so much how we started in the race, but it does matter how we finish.

Shepherd's Crown (or Crown of Glory)

A shepherd's crown is for those who served as faithful pastors. Perhaps God is calling some of you to become a pastor and receive a shepherd's crown. You will know the call deep in your spirit, and people will confirm your call.

> The elders who are among you I exhort, I who am a fellow elder and a witness of the sufferings of Christ, and also a partaker of the glory that will be revealed: Shepherd the flock of God which is among you, serving as overseers, not by compulsion but willingly, not for dishonest gain but eagerly; nor as being lords over those entrusted to you, but being examples to the flock; and when the Chief Shepherd appears, you will receive a crown of glory that does not fade away. (1 Peter 5:1–4 NKJV)

These are sober words to shepherds, but the earthly and heavenly rewards are worth the effort. Faithful pastors who don't often get recognized on earth will be honored in heaven.

In this passage, pastor is from transliteration of the Greek, "Poimen," meaning a shepherd, one who tends herds or flocks (not merely one who feeds them); it is used metaphorically of Christian "pastors" (Eph. 4:11). Pastors guide as well as feed the flock This was also the service committed to elders (overseers, or bishops) (Acts 20:28, 17). These shepherds give tender care and vigilantly superintend the flock.[8]

At the time of Jesus' trial, Peter had denied Jesus three times. When the resurrected Lord addressed Peter, he gently asked three times: "Do you love me?" Each time Peter responded yes. And three times Jesus asked Peter to feed his flock. Twice Jesus said, "Feed my sheep" and once, "Feed my lambs." (John 21:15–17), referring to grown-ups and little ones. Our shepherds should not forget the children. Jesus never did.

What food do the Lord's sheep need? First of all, the written Word. Bible study is vitally important in addition to hearing good sermons. We are also fed through Holy Communion (the Lord's

Supper, the Eucharist, the Mass, or the Covenant Meal), remembering the Lord until he returns.

Prayer, in all its forms, is another must, for it is food for the pastor and flock. Just as Jesus taught his disciples to pray, so it is the joyful responsibility for the pastor to teach his flock to pray. Often pastors are so overworked that it is hard to find time to pray, much less teach their flock to do so. Some helpful courses to help a church grow in its prayer life can be taught by laypeople. I've developed two such courses myself.[9] Alphonsus Ligouri, eighteenth-century bishop, said, "If I had only one sermon to preach, I would preach it on prayer." Obviously he knew the benefits.

Thus, the flock needs a diet of Bible study, inspiring sermons, Holy Communion, and prayer. A faithful shepherd-pastor should read and reread John 10, Jesus' discourse on the Good Shepherd. And pastors would also be wise to have a committed group of intercessors praying for him or her and the pastor's family. Being in the ministry is frontline duty. As pastor, you have a special responsibility to be an example to those who have been entrusted to you. Rest assured that good shepherds (pastors, superintendents, or bishops) will receive a crown of glory that will not fade out of sight.

Crown of Life
Martyr's Crown of Life

Martyrs for Christ are promised a crown of life. No one starts out wanting a crown for this reason, nor should we. We hear of soldiers—fanatical devotees of some religious cause—purposely becoming human bombs, thinking this will give them the better afterlife of a martyr. They are sadly mistaken.

Jesus said, "Be faithful even to the point of death, and I will give you the crown of life" (Rev. 2:10). James says, "Blessed is the man who endures temptation; for when he has been approved, he will receive the crown of life" (1:12 NKJV).

> *They overcame [Satan]*
> *by the blood of the Lamb*

> *and by the word of their testimony;*
> *and they did not love their lives so much*
> *as to shrink from death.*

(Rev. 12:11)

Many have died for the faith—in the Old Testament as well as New, and throughout the church age.

"Martyr" comes from the Greek word *martus*, which means "witness". When you witness an event and are willing to say so, you may be honored—or it may get you into trouble. "The meaning of the word *martyr* which is now the most used, is one who has proved the strength and genuineness of his faith in Christ by undergoing a violent death."[10] In this sense, Stephen, whose death by stoning is recorded in Acts 7:54–60, is listed as the first Christian martyr, but the honor may be contested by John the Baptist, who was beheaded for his faith. (John the Baptist is often considered the last of the Old Testament saints, leaving Stephen [whose name means "crown"] with the "first" distinction in the Christian era.)

Tradition indicates that eleven of the twelve apostles were martyred, John being the exception. This is a very strong witness of the authenticity of the resurrection of Jesus and his divinity. Would all eleven men give their lives for something they knew was a lie? To seal such a commitment with their own blood—surely they were witnesses of the Resurrection.

What is the difference between the death of Jesus Christ and those whose near-death experiences are recounted in this book? These men and women will have to die again, and fortunately they are not afraid to do so. But after Jesus died, he rose from the dead in a new kind of body that is eternal—never to die again. He has a resurrection body—the first of its kind—on a dimension past human knowledge, one that can travel at the speed of light and go through solid walls, one that can eat but doesn't have to, one that is incorruptible. Jesus the Lord promised this kind of body to those who love him; it will be given at the first resurrection of the dead (see Hebrews 11:35, Revelation 20:5). Such knowledge gives courage to those being martyred and to the families left behind.

Another early church martyr was named Antipas. We know virtually nothing about him, though he has traditionally been called the bishop of Pergamos. The book of Revelation records Jesus' message to the church at Pergamos: "And you hold fast to My name, and did not deny My faith even in the days in which Antipas was My faithful martyr, who was killed among you, where Satan dwells" (2:13 NKJV).

Currently there is increased concern about persecution and martyrdom of Christians. Church researcher David Barrett claims that in 1994 there were some 156,000 Christian martyrs worldwide—in Pakistan, Rwanda, Colombia, Iran, Peru, and other countries.[11] We who are living in countries that value religious freedom are often blind to the struggles of the rest of the world.

Corrie ten Boom, a Dutch heroine sent to one of Hitler's concentration camps for hiding Jews, wrote of her experiences in a now-classic book called *The Hiding Place*. In it, she recalls a particular time in her childhood when she was nearly overcome by the fear of dying and being separated from her loved ones. Her father comforted her with these loving and wise words:

> "Corrie," he began gently, "when you and I go to Amsterdam—when do I give you your ticket?"
> I sniffed a few times, considering this.
> "Why, just before we get on the train."
> "Exactly. And our wise Father in heaven knows when we're going to need things, too. Don't run out ahead of Him, Corrie. When the time comes that some of us will have to die, you will look into your heart and find the strength you need— just in time."[12]

That's what happened to all of these brave martyrs: John the Baptist, Stephen, eleven of the apostles, Antipas, Paul, and hundreds of thousands of others. At the last moment they were given the courage. They remained faithful to death, and they will receive a glorious, sparkling crown of life.

I note the lines of a hymn by George Duffield:

> *To him that overcometh,*
> *A crown of life shall be;*
> *He with the King of glory*
> *Shall reign eternally.*

These are the five beautiful crowns God offers. It is interesting that there are five—and five is the number traditionally associated with God's grace, the five wounds of Jesus—in his hands, feet, and side being the greatest example. As I said, crowns and grace go together. Any rewards we receive are through and because of the grace of our Lord. Jesus says, "Behold, I am coming soon! My reward is with me" (Rev. 22:12). He himself is our greatest reward. Without him all rewards would be empty.

Watch Out for Crown Stealers

To the faithful church of Philadelphia, Jesus says, "I am coming soon. Hold on to what you have, so that no one will take your crown" (Rev. 3:11). In this world there are crown stealers. Who are they? Those not interested in the kingdom of God and not wanting you to be either. They want company in their utterly earthly and worldly pursuits.

Crown stealers are people who tempt you with age-old lines: "But everyone is doing it. Just one time won't hurt." Or "Marriage is old-fashioned; you should have gotten over that idea years ago." Or "Everyone is a little dishonest; you can cheat on this contract and no one will know it. Let me show you how."

Wouldn't it be sad to have a crown waiting for you and then allow it to be stolen? We need to be careful about the friends with whom we choose to spend a lot of time. With frequent interaction, it is easy to absorb many of their ways of thinking. These "friends" may be other than human—radio or TV shows, books or magazines, or the internet world all have the potential for misuse.

Kinds of Judgment

At the Olympic games of Athens, Corinth, and other cities, the judge sat on the *bema* seat—the judgment seat. At the judgment seat, after the tournament, the victorious athlete would receive the crown in the form of a wreath, plus other benefits. Robbie Stephens, Bible teacher and friend, told me of her 1980 tour of the ruins of the stadium in Corinth, near Athens. It was exciting, she said, to see the marble platform, or the *bema*, where judgment for early Olympic sports events took place.

Paul speaks of the judgment seat of Christ—the *bema* seat. This judgment seat is not like a judge's chambers where a judge raps the gavel and gives a punitive sentence: "thirty days" or "thirty years," or "life." It is a judgment that results in rewards—or loss of rewards—for believers. This individual review of our workers will cleanse us, leaving us free to rejoice.

A different judgment, called the White Throne Judgment, is described for those who have turned their back on Christ and refused his grace—those whose names are not written in the Lamb's Book of Life (Rev. 20:11). Craig Gottschalk had a preview of this punitive judgment. Craig knew he was rightly judged guilty, but God gave back his life through the powerful intercessory prayers of a grandmother. Because Craig was reborn, his name was written in the Book of Life and he escaped eternal separation from God.

As I said, at this future *bema* judgment, God's children receive appropriate kingly crowns. Here we will also be given personal rewards of gold, silver, and precious stones that survived testing. (In chapter 12 we will learn of the wedding gifts Christ the Bridegroom will give to us, his bride.) Paul describes this judgment:

> For no one can lay any foundation other than the one already laid, which is Jesus Christ. If any man builds on this foundation using gold, silver, costly stones, wood, hay or straw, his work will be shown for what it is, because the Day will bring it to light. It will be revealed with fire, and the fire will test the quality of each man's work. If what he has built survives, he will receive his reward. If it is burned up, he will suffer loss; he himself will be saved, but only as one escaping through the flames. (1 Cor. 3:11–15)

Note that the Scripture is speaking of loss of rewards, not the loss of one's spirit and soul or of one's salvation.

Gold, Silver, Precious Stones

Let me tell you about a few witnesses par excellence, three Olympic medalists who were willing to express their faith publicly. Terry Whalin quotes them in the July 1996 *Charisma* magazine.[13]

David Robinson was part of the 1996 U.S. Olympic basketball "Dream Team" that won the gold medal in Atlanta. Whalin reports: "In 1991 Robinson gave his life completely to Christ. He now understands that being a Christian means a call to responsibility. 'There is a fire that burns inside you when you love the Lord,' he says. 'The message is, do everything to your best and to the glory of God.'"

In 1996 Mike Marsh and his team won the silver medal in the 400-meter relay in track. Mike had won two gold medals in Barcelona. A Christian since 1987, Marsh says, "Hardships help shape you." Whalin comments, "Just as he trains physically for the Olympics, Marsh also trains spiritually. 'The spiritual training also has to be done consistently and on a schedule.'"

Jackie Joyner-Kersee took the bronze medal in the long jump before injuring herself. Whalin notes: "Some people call Joyner-Kersee the world's greatest female athlete. A three-time Olympian, Jackie has distinguished herself in the long jump and heptathlon, a seven-event contest of running, jumping and throwing for which she won the silver medal in 1984 and the gold in 1988 and 1992. She also is known as a committed Christian and often gives her testimony publicly."

Although all three athletes have won gold medals in the course of their careers, in 1996 Robinson received a gold, Marsh a silver, and Joyner-Kersee a bronze. Sounds a lot like the rewards of gold, silver, and precious stones cited in Scripture. In the greatest Olympic game yet to come, David, Mike, and Jackie may well receive the best reward of all—a pure gold crown of rejoicing for souls won by their lives of excellence and their witness, as well as gold, silver, and precious stones from God's own hand.

Writing to believers, Paul said of the *bema* seat: "So we make it our goal to please him, whether we are at home in the body or away from it. For we must all appear before the judgment seat of Christ, that each one may receive what is due him for the things done while in the body, whether good or bad. Since, then, we know what it is to fear [respect] the Lord, we try to persuade men" (2 Cor. 5:9–11).

And in Romans Paul writes: "You, then, why do you judge your brother? Or why do you look down on your brother? For we will all stand before God's judgment seat. . . . So then, each of us will give an account of himself to God" (14:10, 12).

During Lent some Christians make a special effort to work on and pray about their weak areas—what the Bible calls "wood, hay, and stubble." We need to take time to let God search our hearts at this season and at other times also. Do be careful, however, not to get into too much introspection without balancing it with the many positive aspects of your faith.

Sinful behavior would improve quickly if we remembered to do one thing every day: obey Christ's command to love God and others. Jesus said: "'Love the Lord your God with all your heart, soul, and mind.' This is the first and greatest commandment. The second most important is similar: 'Love your neighbor as much as you love yourself.' All the other commandments and all the demands of the prophets stem from these two laws and are fulfilled if you obey them. Keep only these and you will find that you are obeying all the others" (Matt. 22:37–40 TLB).

In chapter 2, I recommended setting our minds on heaven just as we set our clocks for important events—like getting up for work in the morning. The *Amplified Bible* says, "Set your minds and keep them set on what is above" (Col. 3:2). That really means setting your mind on love, for love is the essence of God. It isn't always easy for us to love; we have to choose to do it. Set ourselves to do it. Make it a habit of life. Be a little piece of heaven walking on earth.

At this future day of accounting, I trust that your works and mine won't be too singed around the edges. I take comfort in knowing that this judgment takes place before Jesus Christ, who walked this earth for thirty-three years. He knows the way. He is the Way, and he is the perfect righteous Judge for believers.

In chapter 10 you have already seen a little snapshot of what rejoicing in heaven will be like. Amy Carmichael said, "We have all of eternity to celebrate the victories, and only a few hours before sunset in which to win them."[14] Press on to make a good finish.

See You There

Ruling and reigning with Christ in his kingdom is one of the great rewards God will give his children. If you have studied the

lives of the Old Testament kings of Israel and Judah, you were
probably surprised to find out how poorly they measured up to
God's standards. Out of nineteen kings in Israel, 100 percent were
bad or wicked; and of the twenty kings of Judah, fourteen were
bad—only two were really good. Both kingdoms eventually fell
into captivity as a result of their wrong choices. It is not easy being
a king. Power quickly goes to one's head. Queens, kings, and their
heirs in our day have their problems too.

We'll have to do better than most of those in earth's royalty.
The more faithful you are here, the greater responsibility will be
given you in heaven. This is a race to qualify for greater service
to God.

Rewards for the greatest Olympic game will be given at the
end of this age of grace, at the *bema* judgment seat, when God's
faithful warriors will be gathered for the time of God's affirma-
tions. We will be in awe as we see the rewards given Abraham
and Sarah, Isaac, Jacob, Moses, Joshua, Deborah, Rahab, Joseph,
Isaiah, Ruth, Jonah, Job, Esther, Samuel, King David, King
Hezekiah, Elijah, John the Baptist, Mary and Joseph, the apostles, Paul, and others of the church age. After biblical times, others are too numerous to name. You fill in the blanks. There will
also be many heroes or heroines we've never heard of before.
How awesome it will be to see them receive rewards after being
so mistreated on earth.

How will you and I dare go up to Christ's throne after all
those mighty saints? By God's grace. What is most important is that
you made it. You're there! Salvation is the greatest gift.

Your further blessings will be perhaps the award of an extra
gold crown—or more—and, I trust, after the dross is removed, to
find gold, silver, and precious stones from a life well lived for God.
What great and eternal gifts to receive for all time, equipping you
for service to the King.

For those in Christ, personal judgment has taken place on
earth, so the *bema* judgment will be a time of rejoicing as we've
never seen before. You can picture it being like the glorious closing ceremonies of all the Olympic Games for all time.

I'll meet you at the *bema*—only because of God's amazing
grace!

CHAPTER TWELVE

Heaven's Gifts to Overcomers

Think of stepping on the shore and finding it heaven;
of touching a hand, and finding it God's;
of breathing new air, and finding it celestial;
of waking up in glory, and finding it home.

Don Wyrtzen,
Finally Home

------◆------

Some may be surprised to hear that we will receive gifts in heaven. A young college graduate to whom I recently mentioned this truth was delightfully surprised. The church these days is fascinated by the gifts God has given to equip us here on earth. In fact, numerous tests have been developed to help us discover which gifts we might have. Of such gifts the apostle James says, "Every good and perfect gift is from above, coming down from the Father of the heavenly lights, who does not change like shifting shadows" (1:17). Heaven is the storehouse of all God's good gifts—those for now and those for later.

You have gifts in heaven to look forward to. Why does God want to give you so many gifts? He loves you, and it is his nature to give wonderful things to his children. Just as you love giving gifts to your children, so does he.

The first part of the book of Revelation includes letters written to the seven churches in Asia, where the apostle John was pastor (or bishop). Each letter contains a commendation from Christ, a reproof, and an exhortation. At the end of each letter to the seven churches, there is a word to the overcomers. All these churches read the letters sent to the others. So they, as we, could read the entire message to overcomers. The Greek word here for overcomer is *nikao*, meaning to "conquer, overcome, prevail, get the victory."[1]

Here is what John says elsewhere in his epistle, "For everyone born of God overcomes the world. This is the victory that has overcome the world, even our faith. Who is it that overcomes the world? Only he who believes that Jesus is the Son of God" (1 John 5:4–5). Here the truth is made plain—you can be an overcomer if you so choose.

From these Revelation "overcomer notes," we can get a further glimpse of the heavenly gifts Christ will give to those who are faithful and obedient to him.

1. Fruit from the Tree of Life

"He who has an ear, let him hear what the Spirit says to the churches. To him who overcomes, I will give to eat from the tree of life, which is in the midst of the Paradise of God" (Rev. 2:7 NKJV).

In the Garden of Eden, the Tree of Life meant perpetual physical and spiritual life. In disobeying God by eating the fruit of another tree, the Tree of the Knowledge of Good and Evil, Adam and Eve were sent away from Eden and its perfection. The human life span was limited; humanity tasted of physical and spiritual death. But in heaven, believers will eat from the fruit of the Tree of Life—not for healing, longevity, and restoration but for enjoyment, vitality, and inspiration, plus things we don't know about yet. What powerful food it must be. In God's grace we enter back into what humankind lost in the Garden, and yet heaven is beyond that state.

2. Eternal Life with God

"He who overcomes will not be hurt at all by the second death" (Rev. 2:11).

The second death is a place of eternal separation from God, the One who loves you most. There is no good reason why any person needs to spend an eternity separated from God. *Gehenna*, or hell, was not created for humans but for the deceiver, Satan, and his evil spirits who made war with God. But men and women who turn their back on Christ to the end will not spend eternity in the presence of God.

In chapter 8 Lorraine Tutmarc said, "When I saw all that water, I knew I was dying. And when this voice told me I was lost and this was eternity, then I knew God was revealing to me my lost condition. . . . In pain, misery, and fear, I kept sinking down into this water. When I got down to the bottom, I couldn't fight anymore. Completely exhausted, I gave up. Then I saw light enter the water around me." We know the rest of her wonderful story and how she became an overcomer through meeting Jesus Christ. At that time she received the down payment—Scripture calls it the "deposit guaranteeing our inheritance" (Eph. 1:14)—for the gift she received in full when she entered heaven after her death in 1992. "Having believed, you were sealed with the Holy Spirit of promise, who is the guarantee of our inheritance" (Eph. 1:13–14).

The saying goes, "If you're born twice, you'll die once; if you're born once, you'll die twice." A believer has only one death, and "whosoever will" come to Christ is welcomed into God's eternal kingdom. Be very sure that you have a heavenly birthday as well as an earthly one. You may not believe in such an entity as Satan, but don't let that issue (does he or does he not exist?) keep you from making a commitment to Jesus. Receive Jesus with your heart and then ask the Holy Spirit to reveal truth to you.

Overcomers have already received this gift of deliverance from the second death, which is separation from God forever, and will experience the full joy of their deliverance in heaven. The two kinds of death, physical and spiritual—due to man's original fall—were conquered at the cross. Physical death for the Christian is like what the psalmist describes: "Though I walk through the valley of the shadow of death . . . you are with me" (Ps. 23:4). Death is only a shadow, and then we're immediately drawn into God's marvelous light.

3. Hidden Manna and a White Stone

"To him who overcomes, I will give some of the hidden manna. I will also give him a white stone with a new name written on it, known only to him who receives it" (Rev. 2:17).

How wonderful it will be to eat of the hidden manna. You've probably read about the children of Israel's forty-year trek across the desert. Manna, their staple food, was provided directly by God. Exodus 16:14 says, "Upon the face of the wilderness there lay a small round thing" (KJV). It seemed to fall with the dew. The Israelites had to be there early to collect their daily portion, as it melted with the heat of the sun. We don't know what this substance was, nor did the Israelites. Clarke says, "It seems to have been created for the present occasion, and like him whom it typified, to have been the only thing of the kind, the only bread from heaven, which God ever gave to preserve the life of man, as Christ is the true bread that came down from heaven, and was given for the life of the world."[2] Scripture says manna "was like white coriander seed, and the taste of it was like wafers made with honey" (Ex. 16:31 NKJV).

When manna is given to you from the supply God has in heaven, it will denote his faithfulness to you as well as to the Israelites. Eating the manna that he gives will be like partaking of the bread of Holy Communion. The Bread of Life himself will be the Great High Priest giving you the bread.

And "white stones with a new name"? To the ancients, a white stone had some legal symbolism. If a judge gave you a white stone, you were pardoned, not condemned. In Roman times they had another significance. Victory stones, or white stones inscribed with the winner's name, were presented to victors at major sports events, such as the Olympics. A white stone entitled you to lifelong public financial support. This is one of the great meanings of the heavenly white stone, as is provision of personal needs.[3] In essence it means that God is going to take care of you at his expense eternally. Having your name engraved on the stone must be incredibly healing. Every time you look at it you are reminded that you are pardoned, provided for, and loved without end.

I don't know all that your new name will mean, but by God's grace you have acquired one that is "child of God." The white stone you receive will show your new name, and no one can fully understand what "child of God" means to you personally. Won't it be wonderful to see what new name Jesus will give you?

4. Reigning Authority and the Morning Star

"To him who overcomes and does my will to the end, I will give authority over the nations—'He will rule them. . .'—just as I have received from my Father. I will also give him the morning star" (Rev. 2:26–28).

You and I as overcomers will assist Christ in his eternal reign: "And they will reign for ever and ever" (Rev. 22:5). "They" in this verse speaks of the Lamb of God and his bondservants, his victorious ones, reigning together. We will assist in judging people and angels; we will train those who have more limited knowledge of God's ways—heaven's lifestyle; and do many other good works he will show us at that time.

The promise of this gift is to the *nikao*, the overcomer, the victorious, the "one who does [God's] will to the end." We need to exhort ourselves to do God's will to the end. It is easy to get sloppy in our faith and just coast along.

During our mature years, we have more to give. Older believers are often wiser from their experience and years of walking with God. An older woman on a TV program was asked if she wished she were young again. Without hesitation she said, "Yes, if I could take my sixty-one-year-old brain with me!"

Even if immobile, one can be an intercessor, encourager, prayer minister, or lead a home Bible class. One Denver woman in her eighties, using a walker, impressed me. At church, people flocked around her as she prayed for the sick and counseled young adults. She will be a good king one day. All of us, including this woman, are in training now.

"I will give him the morning star." Morning Star speaks of Jesus. "I am the Root and the Offspring of David, and the bright Morning Star," says Jesus in Revelation 22:16. He is giving you himself. His starlike quality will shine in your eyes and countenance forever.

Jesus the Morning Star precedes the rising sun of the new day—that future reign of Christ and his people—dawning perhaps sooner than we think.

How do you like your gifts? You'll have not only a crown but the authority that goes with it. You'll work directly under Christ's command. And most of all, he will give you his shining self, the glory of his presence—the Morning Star.

5. *White Garments, Book of Life, and Name Acknowledged*

"He who overcomes will, like them [a few from the church of Sardis], be dressed in white. I will never cross out his name from the book of life, but will acknowledge his name before my Father and his angels" (Rev. 3:5).

The white linen garments represent our cleansed souls, our imputed righteousness. "The Hebrews considered holiness as the garb of the soul, and evil actions as stains or spots on this garb."[4] This robe also represents the wedding garment each person must wear at the wedding of Christ the King (Matt. 22:11–12).

We are not worthy in ourselves, but because of God's grace, no believing Gentile or Hebrew will be without a robe, which will have been cleansed by the perfect cleansing fluid, the blood of Jesus. The important thing is to be sure we are found faithful and that we respond to Jesus while we have time. The matter is not beyond us, for all we're asked to do is trust like little children.

At the World Prayer Congress meeting in Jerusalem, I got a glimpse of what it will be like to receive a white robe in heaven.[5] Before we rallied to march and pray on the walls of the Old City, a ceremony was held in which each person placed a chasuble-like priestly garment over the head and clothing of another. Then a white sash was tied around the waist. All was done with prayer to keep ourselves unspotted from the world. I sensed this was like experiencing Jesus covering us with his robe of righteousness. The next bit of heaven was walking down the Mount of Olives with hundreds of believers of many different races, clad in white garments, headed for the walls of the Old City.

You recall how Dr. Landry said, "I saw saints, souls that were in heaven—multitudes. There was no way to count them. Whether there were millions or billions, I have no idea. As far as I could see in every direction were people dressed in white robes, all sizes." What an awesome sight!

The overcomer will never be blotted out of the Book of Life. Here in heaven you are safe, and you've kept true to the Lord Jesus Christ to the end of your life (Matt. 24:13). One of the most incredible experiences will be to hear Jesus confess your name before his Father, and the saints and angels. If we are faithful to him, the Lord Jesus will say to his Father, "I know him [or her]. This is my friend who loves me." If you confess him now, he will not only confess you now, but also later (Rom. 10:9). That is a covenant relationship sealed in his blood. He will never go back on you. Any breaking of the relationship on earth has to be on your part.

6. Pillar in the Temple

"Him who overcomes I will make a pillar in the temple of my God. Never again will he leave it. I will write on him the name of my God and the name of the city of my God, the new Jerusalem, which is coming down out of heaven from my God; and I will also write on him my new name" (Rev. 3:12).

When I introduce Tom and Mary Murphy to visitors at my church, I often say, "These people are pillars of this church." They respond by laughing and saying humble things like, "Oh no, we're just doing what we can to help." The Murphys are there to assist with landscaping, greet newcomers at the door, usher, or pour coffee after the service. You name it, and they've probably done it during their twenty-one-year membership. Any Christian organization must have people who are pillars—chief supporters who provide strength.

God looks on this support ministry highly and honors believers with the gift of being pillars in his holy temple. If you've enjoyed being a pillar in an earthly church, just think of how great it will be to have this privilege in God's perfect church above.

Being a pillar in God's temple doesn't mean that you will be stationary in a negative sense. "There is probably an allusion here to the two pillars in the temple of Jerusalem, called Jachin and Boaz, meaning stability and strength. The Church is the temple; Christ is the foundation on which it is built; and his ministers are the Pillars by which, under him, it is adorned and supported."[6]

"His name will be on their foreheads" (Rev. 22:4). Jesus' name represents what he is like and that we shall become more and more like him without losing our own identity. His name also shows ownership. He knows who are his. In God's kingdom we are not marked with a number like so many cattle, but we are sealed with Jesus' own dear name. We're sealed also with the name of New Jerusalem—our homeland—and the Holy Spirit, as we saw in the second gift. This is a threefold seal on our lives. What a sense of security this gives us!

7. Throne Privileges

"To him who overcomes, I will give the right to sit with me on my throne, just as I overcame and sat down with my Father on his throne" (Rev. 3:21).

We have already discussed the awesome majesty of God's throne. Jesus is sitting with the Father on the throne to the Father's right; the thrones are as one, even as Father and Son are one. And there in that scene you are welcomed. Jesus wants all the best for you. When you experience a beautiful sunset, an inspiring song, or a lovely dinner, you want the person you love to experience that with you. In this greatest of honors, Jesus wants you beside him. As faithful overcomers we will sit on that same throne. This means we will rule from this position of authority.

One day Jesus' disciples were having a debate about who would sit at the right and left of his throne. Jesus said, "To sit at my right or left is not for me to grant. These places belong to those for whom they have been prepared by my Father" (Matt. 20:23). The disciples didn't understand that Jesus' reign as King of Kings would come later at a totally new dimension than earthly kingdoms. Nor did they realize there would not be two extra seats there, but that a many-membered body would rule and reign from that position on a spiritual level. But then we wouldn't have understood either—two thousand years ago before the canon of Scripture was completed.

Paul's letter to the Ephesians shows us that spiritually we are seated in heavenly places right now due to our new birthright. But one day we will be there to see with our own eyes and experience all that it means to be invited to sit with Jesus on his glorious throne. What could be greater?

8. *Super Gift: Inheriting New Jerusalem*

The entire book of Revelation concludes with another over-comers' reward: "He who overcomes shall inherit all things, and I will be his God and he will be My son" (21:7 NKJV). A major part of your inheritance will be the New Jerusalem, which this verse refers back to, and the personal home there that God has prepared for you. Any property you own on earth will look mighty small in comparison to this heavenly real-estate.

In the parable of the prodigal son, the father says to the elder, responsible son, who is complaining that he is not getting enough: "You are always with me, and everything I have is yours." Due to ignorance, the elder son lived far below his privileges (see Luke 15:11–32). God says to you, "Everything I have is yours." You are coheirs with Christ, the Son of God. All that God has is yours for eternity, and that includes the New Jerusalem and the universe. With this knowledge, you have no more reason to hang your head and go around feeling devalued or impoverished.

The greatest gift of all is when God says, "I will be his God and he will be my son." *Son* (Gk. *huios*) here means a maturing person (male or female). A son has grown up and become a mature child. This is a person with whom the Father can share his heart and entrust his treasures. One of your goals on earth, and obvi-ously in heaven, is to grow up "unto the measure of the stature of the fullness of Christ" (Eph. 4:13 KJV). How wonderful to reach your full potential in Christ. I think, too, you'll always have the childlike quality that Jesus says is required to enter the kingdom of God (Matt. 18:3). To be claimed as God's own child is the ulti-mate gift. You entered into this gift while on earth, but in heaven you will experience it in full. Praise him!

Amazing Grace

Our efforts and strivings to be deemed fit to receive God's crowns and gifts should always be balanced out with God's grace. I reiterate: No one can ever make oneself good enough to earn heaven. As sons and daughters of Adam and Eve we are sinners. Sin means going our own way instead of God's way (Isa. 53:6). It means missing the mark of perfection. You will never be able to keep the Ten Commandments perfectly—in thought if not in action.

You can never pay for your sins, which separate you from the holy triune God, though you may try to "pay" for your sins as you pay off a debt. Think of it this way: Say you're a big spender trying to pay off a credit card bill. When the bill comes around, you pay the minimum amount due and then keep on spending. You need a loan? Just borrow credit from the "never-ending" bank supply. Temptation is everywhere to lure you into overuse. But eventually you realize that on your meager salary you will never be able to pay off this debt and its interest. Each month that you don't pay off your entire bill, the cost of your loan goes up, up, up. You realize you're going to lose everything—your house, your car, your mate. And to top it off, you end up in jail!

Then one day you meet a man who has a heart of mercy, one who offers to pay your debt as well as your prison bail. You can't believe this good news. With tears in your eyes, you tell him you can never pay him back.

He smiles and says, "I know; that's why I'm here. I came to show you God's amazing grace. One day through God's Word I found that Jesus Christ, the Son of God, came to pay all my old debts and to bail me out of my inner prison of addictions, loneliness, and depression. My debts were beyond what I could ever afford to pay. Jesus said, 'I've come to heal the brokenhearted, to proclaim liberty to the captives ... to set at liberty those who are oppressed' (Luke 4:18 NKJV). He did that for me, and I'm passing along to you the good news of his grace and mercy. I hope you'll follow my example by inviting him to pay your inner bills. In our own selves we can do nothing when it comes to saving ourselves."

This parable reminds us of our total dependency on God. As we consider God's gifts we need to always be aware of his grace. Yet there is no reason why we, as God's children, shouldn't rejoice in God's gifts and rewards.

I was once an elementary school teacher, and I know that children need praise for jobs well done. Rewards help children to continue to excel. They need certificates of achievement or badges to sew on their sleeves. God, the best Teacher of all, is motivating us to do our best for him, and at the same time giving us joy. Through these treasures God is attempting to make us into his image and likeness. He is drawing us with his love.

Rewards and overcomers' gifts make me want to gear up my Olympic training. How about you? Do you have your training clothes on? Don't just veg out as a couch potato. Remember, you always feel better after you exercise. Let's get into some spiritual muscle-pumping, blood-circulating, mind-energizing training. Are you going for the gold?

CHAPTER THIRTEEN

Your Heavenly Wedding

I am going now to prepare a place for you, and after I have gone and prepared you a place, I shall return to take you with me.

Jesus Christ, Bridegroom,
John 14:1–3 (JB)

———◆———

The book of Revelation describes a "marriage supper of the Lamb"—a future marriage celebration at which Jesus is the Bridegroom, and you and I—his church—are the bride. In chapter 10 we pictured believers entering heaven individually at the time of death. Now we will look at the many-membered bride entering heaven together; this will be another glimpse of the celestial city with a different emphasis. Of this time of the wedding, Jesus promised us, "I will come back and take you to be with me" (John 14:3). In this chapter I share how I imagine preparations for the wedding and the wedding itself will unfold. Again, note that the language in heaven is beyond gender. First a short discussion about marriage itself.

When God gave instructions on how husbands and wives were to live together to reach their fullest potential and joy, he had a double purpose. First God wanted a family, and that family needed to grow and fill the earth. For a man and a woman—two independent human beings—to come together in a happy, long marriage, there needed to be lots of love on three dimensions: *agape* (spirit), *phileo* (soul), and *eros* (body). The fruit of such a marriage is usually offspring.

The second reason, which is really first in God's omniscient viewpoint, is to teach you and me about the relationship between the Bridegroom Jesus Christ and his bride—the church. Earthly marriage is on a three-dimensional level, but heaven's marriage is on a level beyond all known dimensions. The picture of marriage is a shorthand way for God to get an idea across to us. In Ephesians 5:22–33 Paul describes in detail what the married life of emotionally whole couples should be like. In verse 32 he gives the bottom line: "This is a profound mystery—but I am talking about Christ and the church."

I think so many fiery darts are aimed at couples because marriage has a higher purpose than what we presently know. Marriage is a picture of your commitment to Christ on the deepest possible level of union and communion, and of life with him eternally. On earth a good marriage is like a little bit of heaven.

To couples deeply in love it is hard to think of heaven not including the love and ecstasy of marriage. In your present marital bliss I would advise you to pull out all the stops, give it all you've got, because it will be different after this life. "But can it get better?" Yes, and God would say, "Come up higher from earthly to heavenly thinking." The ecstasy of heaven's marriage with Christ is as different as a drop of water and an ocean, or a paint-by-number picture and a Rembrandt.

Bride or *son* or *king* is a shorthand way of telling a whole story in a few words. Men should not feel uncomfortable that they will be considered part of "the bride of Christ." In heaven *bride* doesn't mean being feminine as we know the word; it is beyond earthly concepts. To see what Jesus means about the bride and Bridegroom relationship, look at the Ephesians 5:22–33 passage about marriage in my paraphrase showing Christ as the Bridegroom.

> Dear bride, submit yourself to the Bridegroom; he is your Lord, your King. The Bridegroom is the head of the bride; he is the head of the church and the Savior of the body. The church is subject to Christ in every way—spirit, soul, and body. The Bridegroom loves his bride so much that he died for her, that through his death he might sanctify and cleanse her with the washing of water through the word. That he

might present her to himself a glorious church, not having spot, or wrinkle, or any such thing; but that she should be holy and without blemish. So the Bridegroom loves his bride as his own body. No bridegroom ever hated his own body, but nourishes and cherishes it, for this Bridegroom is Jesus Christ. You are a member of his body, of his flesh, and of his bones. For this reason the bride shall leave all others and be joined to her Bridegroom, and the two shall be one. The Bridegroom loves his bride even as himself. The bride delights in showing reverence for her Husband. This is speaking of the great mystery of Christ and his church.

The Jewish Wedding

One cannot understand the wedding of Christ and the plans for our future except through the children of Israel. When Jesus became God incarnate through the Virgin Mary, he joined himself to the Jewish race. Because Jesus was born and raised a Jew, the Jewish wedding would be a most appropriate type and shadow of his marriage to come.

Jesus never had a wedding on earth, nor was that his intention, though marriage was "expected." "For the young man of Israel, to be married, bear children, and assume his responsibilities in the Jewish community were the prime goals of his life. From the time of his Bar Mitzvah at age thirteen until about age twenty is the time in which he would be expected to take a wife."[1] At age thirty-three Jesus died a single person. He certainly didn't fit into the average Jewish structure. But he was not a regular man with earthly plans; he was God made flesh with eternal plans. Jesus performed his first miracle at the wedding at Cana near Nazareth, possibly looking forward to his own wedding in heaven to his bride, the church—those who have turned to him as their Lord and Savior.

Arrangements for a Jewish wedding were made by an agent or matchmaker working on behalf of the potential groom's father, or possibly by the groom himself or a friend of the groom. The young man—the aspiring bridegroom—prepared himself to go to the house of the potential bride to meet her father; in hand he had a contract and the purchase price for the bride. Polly Perkins says,

"The match maker was considered to be doing God's work as it is believed that marriages are made in heaven."[2] In Scripture we see Eliezer as the agent for Abraham's son Isaac in wooing Rebekah (Gen. 24). Many biblical teachers see Eliezer as a type of the Holy Spirit who comes to earth to call a bride for God's only Son, Jesus.

In a Jewish setting the negotiations might have gone something like this. Say Joel, a friend of both the father and Joshua, the son, agrees to be the son's agent. Joel sets up an appointment and visits with the young woman's father, telling him every good thing he knows about his friend. The woman's father is impressed and an appointment is set for the potential groom to come visit. With anticipation Joshua comes bringing three things: a good sum of money to pay the bride price, a betrothal contact, and a skin of wine. They meet, and yes, there is immediate rapport. During the visit the contract is laid out, the price is discussed, and a cup of wine is poured.

If the young man's offer is acceptable, the woman's father calls in his daughter. If she drinks the wine, she indicates that she has accepted this man to be her husband. They drink from the cup together, sealing the marriage covenant. In essence, they're saying, "The life is in the blood, and now as we drink this cup of wine together, my life and your life are becoming one."[3] They are now committed to one another. The betrothal is as binding as the marriage itself. From this point on they are called husband and wife. Their union can be dissolved only by divorce, but they do not have conjugal rights until the actual wedding.

After the betrothal a bride is set apart by wearing a veil over her face when she goes out in public. From this time on the bridegroom may come at any time to receive his bride. The tradition is to come at night, especially at midnight. The bridegroom is busy preparing a new home and the bridal chamber *(chadar)* for her.

Each night the bride trims and lights her lamp to show that she is ready and waiting. The groom checks with his father for the appropriate time to get his bride. At that exciting moment, the groom gathers together his groomsmen. They head for the bride's house; when they're nearly there one of them shouts to warn her of their imminent arrival. She has a few minutes to get herself ready to leave her father's house. Her attendants hear the cry also.

Bride and groom meet dressed in their wedding garments. With their attendants they head for the groom's father's house for wedding vows and a short ceremony. A second contract, containing promises the groom pledges to his wife, is given to her parents.

The bride and groom then enter their chambers for a sevenday honeymoon. These are called "days of hiding." He removes her veil and knows her secrets. The best man actually stands by the door to know when the bride and groom have come together, and the groom calls through the door to let him be first to know of their union. John the Baptist made reference to this part of the ritual: "He who has the bride is the bridegroom; but the friend of the bridegroom, who stands and hears him, rejoices greatly because of the bridegroom's voice. Therefore this joy of mine is fulfilled" (John 3:29 NKJV). Then the wedding party—family and friends—celebrates during those seven days.

John's account of Jesus' first miracle at the wedding in Cana indicates that this wedding party had been celebrating three days when the host ran out of wine. To remedy the situation Jesus turned six huge pots of water into wine. The best wine!

When the honeymoon is over, the groom brings his wife from their *chadar* with her veil removed. He introduces his bride to the wedding party, they are greeted with great cheers, and then the final great wedding feast takes place.

Here you get a taste of how a Jewish wedding might have been planned when Jesus was living as a man on earth. Let's make a few parallels about the future heavenly wedding of Christ. Our wedding.

Your Heavenly Wedding

As I came to understand elements of the ancient Jewish wedding, I could see parallels in Revelation and in other parts of the Bible to the marriage of the Lamb. The following scenario is not complete, and of course it is my interpretation, but here's how I see it.

Jesus has chosen you for his own. He and his Father have sent the Holy Spirit to tell you of his love, to draw you to him. The wedding contract is the New Testament. The purchase price for you, his bride, was Jesus' own blood. Paul sees this when he writes, "You are not your own; you were bought at a price. Therefore honor God with your body" (1 Cor. 6:19–20).

Paul quotes Jesus as saying: "'This cup is the new covenant in My blood. This do, as often as you drink it, in remembrance of Me.' For as often as you eat this bread and drink this cup, you proclaim the Lord's death till He comes" (1 Cor. 11:25–26 NKJV). Jesus saw that you accepted his invitation—his betrothal offer—when you welcomed him into your life (which includes baptism), and when at your first Communion you picked up the cup of wine (fruit of the vine), his blood, and drank it. You have a covenant relationship with him. By drinking the cup you said, "Yes, Lord, I accept you as my Bridegroom. I'm betrothed (engaged and more) to you. I'll love you forever." Every time you receive the cup at Communion, you know he is thinking of you and loves you. From now on you are set apart by the Lord; you wear the anointing of the Holy Spirit as a covering over your life. This is a covering of joy as well as protection. "You anoint my head with oil; my cup runs over" (Ps. 23:5 NKJV).

Looking toward the marriage day, Jesus says to you: "In my Father's house are many rooms; if it were not so, I would have told you. I am going there to prepare a place for you. And if I go and prepare a place for you, I will come back and take you to be with me that you also may be where I am" (John 14:2–3). Jesus spoke these words at the significant Passover meal the night before he was slain. It was like the speech a Jewish bridegroom would make before he left to prepare their new home. Jesus here was speaking to his bride, his disciples, which now includes you and me. Your residence-to-be is in the New Jerusalem, the sparkling city.

Over these last two thousand years Jesus has been looking forward daily to his wedding. The wedding will not take place when any one of us naturally dies and goes to heaven but at the time described here by Paul: "I tell you a mystery: We will not all sleep [in death], but we will all be changed [transformed]—in a flash, in the twinkling of an eye, at the last trumpet. For the trumpet will sound, the dead [in Christ] will be raised imperishable, and we will be changed" (1 Cor. 15:51–52).

At the time of the sounding of that trumpet (*shofar*), some of us may already be enjoying the delights of heaven. Having died, our spirits may be there without our glorified, resurrected bodies. In heaven we will be anticipating this day when our bodies will be resurrected, transformed, glorified. Those on earth will watch for our Bridegroom's coming. "Blessed are those servants whom the master, when he comes, will find watching" (Luke 12:37 NKJV). But until the sound of that trumpet, those in heaven and on earth will eagerly await the call.

The Bridegroom may come at any moment to receive his bride. He is now at his Father's house preparing a bridal chamber and building on new rooms to enlarge the glorious house. Only the Father knows when preparations have been fully made for the bride and for the wedding. Jesus said, "But of that day and hour no one knows, not even the angels of heaven, but my Father only" (Matt. 24:36 NKJV).

The apostle Paul again uses bridal imagery: "I am jealous for you with a godly jealousy. I promised you to one husband, to Christ, so that I might present you as a pure virgin to him" (2 Cor. 11:2).

And in Revelation, John writes: "Let us be glad and rejoice and give Him glory, for the marriage of the Lamb has come, and His wife has made herself ready. And to her it was granted to be arrayed in fine linen, clean and bright, for the fine linen is the righteous acts of the saints" (Rev. 19:7–8 NKJV).

As you, the bride, wait for the Lord to return for you, you keep yourself pure by studying in his Book the love letters and the many messages that instruct you in life's lessons, by talking to the Father and the Groom through prayer, by keeping morally and spiritually pure, by inviting others to the wedding, by learning how to be a good spouse, by having Communion in remembrance of him. The length of your waiting period is unknown.

In a Jewish wedding it takes about a year to complete the marriage preparation. For our spiritual marriage to Christ, it may be a lifetime. But while waiting, the bride of Christ looks to the signs of the times and compares them with God's Word marking encouraging signposts. The important fact is that the wedding will take place in God's time.

Beautiful verses from Malachi show what we are doing while waiting, and God's loving response: "Then those who feared the LORD spoke often to one another: and the LORD heard it, and a book of remembrance was written before him for those who feared the LORD, and thought on his name. And they shall be mine, says the LORD of hosts, in that day when I make up my jewels; and I will spare them, as a man spares his own son who serves him" (3:16–17 KJV modernized).

A groom usually comes at midnight, or sometimes earlier—but one never knows exactly when—so as the bride, you keep a ready supply of oil and your lights trimmed and lit on the chance he might come tonight. You are ready to leave on a moment's notice. The attendants are ready also, as well as all those dear to you. You don't want anyone left out, so you keep inviting people to join you at the wedding.

Your fine linen wedding garments are ready and being adorned further each day. The seed pearls of lives won for the King are being added to the veil. The acts of kindness, helping the needy, healing the wounded, are creating transparent gold border to frame the front of your royal robe of righteousness. The jewels for your neck and hands look more and more like the sardis, emerald, sapphire, amethyst, and other gemstones on the walls of heaven. Each night you look out the window and think, *Maybe tonight.* When you awaken in the morning you think, *This might be the day.*

You remember the words of Isaiah:

> *I will greatly rejoice in the LORD,*
> *My soul shall be joyful in my God;*
> *For He has clothed me with the garments of salvation,*
> *He has covered me with the robe of righteousness,*
> *As a bridegroom decks himself with ornaments,*
> *And as a bride adorns herself with her jewels.*

(61:10 NKJV)

The Groom checks with his Father for the right time to get his bride. When the moment arrives, he calls the friends of the Groom to come with him, the archangel—perhaps Gabriel—to warn the bride, and the shofar trumpet blower, plus maybe Michael the warrior archangel, and perhaps John the Baptist as best man. The bride will have a very brief time to get ready to leave—not minutes but nanoseconds, the blink of an eye.

> *My lover spoke and said to me,*
> *"Arise, my darling,*
> *my beautiful one, and come with me.*
> *See! The winter is past;*
> *the rains are over and gone.*
> *Flowers appear on the earth;*
> *the season of singing has come,*
> *the cooing of doves*
> *is heard in our land.*
> *The fig tree forms its early fruit;*
> *the blossoming vines spread their fragrance.*
> *Arise, come, my darling;*
> *my beautiful one, come with me."*
>
> (Song of Songs 2:10–13)

"After this I looked, and there before me was a door standing open in heaven. And the voice I had first heard speaking to me like a trumpet said, 'Come up here'" (Rev. 4:1). God is calling John to come, but he is calling us also.

Then one evening you actually hear the shout, "Arise, my bride! Come away with me!" This is the moment you've been waiting for! Then there's another shout, this time from the archangel: "Behold, the Bridegroom! Come out to meet him!" (Matt. 25:6 NASB). Next there's a long trumpet blast from the shofar. Two shouts and a trumpet blast; the dead raised, the living changed, the call home.

The anointing of the Holy Spirit falls upon you. It is as if a bolt of power hits you from the top of your head to your toes. Every cell is vibrating as gravity loses its grip on you. You feel yourself rising, you look down and see the tops of trees and houses. You look up and see the Bridegroom glowing and radiant with his

Shechinah glory clouds around him. Multitudes are rising in the sky as his many-membered bride. All in white wedding garments, they are drawn to him like a magnet. Angels are singing hallelu-jahs. Jesus' love reaches out to everyone individually. Traveling at the speed of light or thought, in no time at all you're at the apex of the universe. The light of the heavenly city is the most glorious light you've ever seen, yet it doesn't hurt your eyes.

You arrive at the magnificent wall and gate of pearl. People pour in on every side. All twelve gates are very busy. You're awestruck by it all. If you have time, you notice the inscribed names of those honored and you think, "How wonderful, I'll look at it more closely later." The watchful angel understands. Every-one is rejoicing, and you're meeting family and friends not seen for scores of years. Saints who have died before you are united with their resurrected bodies. It's like the best family reunions or school reunions you've been to—all put together in one event.

As you enter, you are overwhelmed because the New Jerusalem is the fulfillment of the Holy of Holies in the earthly Jerusalem temple. You realize you are standing in a massive Holy of Holies.

At the appropriate moment, from his throne Jesus welcomes the bride and tells each of us of his love and how he has longed for this moment. He lets us know we are worth his every sacrifice—his ultimate sacrifice. His joyful eyes look directly into yours—and mine; he smiles a tender smile, and you tremble at the power of his love. You notice that others are sensing this same experience.

Remembering the Scripture you loved and thought about dur-ing your time of waiting you softly repeat,

> *For your Maker is your husband—*
> *the LORD Almighty is his name—*
> *the Holy One of Israel is your Redeemer;*
> *he is called the God of all the earth.*
>
> (Isa. 54:5)

You're awed by his majesty and his throne; the fragrance of myrrh, aloes, and cassia fills the air, mingling with the joy of his laughter.

Your throne, O God, will last for ever and ever;
  a scepter of justice will be the scepter of your kingdom.
You love righteousness and hate wickedness;
  therefore God, your God, has set you above your
    companions
  by anointing you with the oil of joy.
All your robes are fragrant with myrrh and aloes
    and cassia;
  from palaces adorned with ivory
  the music of the strings makes you glad.
Daughters of kings are among your honored women;
  at your right hand is the royal bride in gold of Ophir.

                                              (Ps. 45:6–9)

Right then and there the marriage takes place. The bride is covered by the canopy of God's love. The New Testament, marriage contract, in Jesus' blood, has already been given. The Father stands and says, "This is my Son, whom I love; with him I am well pleased" (Matt. 3:17). "And, to my children, my sons and daughters,"

Yes, I have loved you
  with an everlasting love;
Therefore with lovingkindness
  I have drawn you.

                            (Jer. 31:3 NKJV)

He asks if the bride of every nation, race, and tongue will take Jesus Christ for her wedded Husband. The multitudes shout, "Hallelujah, I do!" The Groom and bride are pronounced Husband and wife. Cheers go up like thunder.

Jesus told his disciples following their last supper together, "I tell you, I will not drink of this fruit of the vine from now on until that day when I drink it anew with you in my Father's kingdom" (Matt. 26:29). When he reminds us of his words, we now realize what he meant two millenia ago. What incredible fulfillment for all of us. Dr. Amos Millard, with whom I have had many inspiring conversations, says "Christian Communion comes out of the Passover meal, where there were four cups of wine poured: sanctification, judgment, redemption, and the cup of Elijah (Exod. 12:12–14) The third cup, which was served with unleavened bread, was appropriately called the Cup of Redemption, or Kingdom Blessing, and is the one from which Jesus instituted at the last Supper." Jesus will serve us the bread and wine portion of the covenant meal, which is the fulfillment and culmination of what we have been doing on earth. Passover was a meal centered in the home, and we have come home.

Taking bread in his nail-pierced hands, Jesus says, "Take and eat; this is my body" (Matt. 26:26). As the unleavened bread is passed out, it seems to multiply as with the feeding of the multitudes on earth. A murmur of praise washes over and over the crowd like ocean waves. We partake and feel so at one with him and with one another. We are truly one in the Spirit just as we had often prayed to be. The unity is incredible; we bask in it for a while. No one wants to move.

Jesus, Lamb of God, lifts the cup of redemption and blesses it. "Then he took the cup, gave thanks and offered it to them, saying, 'Drink from it, all of you. This is my blood of the covenant, which is poured out for many for the forgiveness of sins'" (Matt. 26:27-28). We are served by the many saints, known and unknown, who followed him faithfully while on earth. We partake. A hush falls on the bride; she sways with the impact of the moment. You reflect, "This is his life poured out for me on the cross! 'I am my beloved's and he is mine'—for eternity [Song of Sol. 6:3 KJV]. His grace and *agape* love are incredible. They are as deep as the deepest ocean, as high as the highest galaxy, as wide as many universes. I've never known him this completely before! It will be centuries before I can begin to take it in."

Jesus looks endearingly at his Father, then at his bride, and says, "As You, Father, are in Me and I in You," they are one in us (John 17:21 AMP). Now more than ever you are truly one with the triune God: Christ in the Father, you in Christ, and he in you.

Gifts Given

When everyone is nourished and has finished passing the kiss of peace, the *shalom*, from one to the other, Jesus calls us to the *bema seat*, his throne. We then receive one or more crowns—watcher's crown, soul-winner's crown, crown of purity, shepherd's crown, crown of life—plus gold, silver, and precious stones of good works, and/or words of loving encouragement, such as, "Well done, good and faithful servant! You have been faithful with a few things; I will put you in charge of many things" (Matt. 25:23). What a time of awesome wonder! Obviously, this will be greater than any Olympic award ceremony ever held on earth.

Jesus lets us know that his plans for us will be revealed before we go back to earth with him to reign at his second advent. For now, there will be the honeymoon where we will get more deeply acquainted with him and with one another. The Father beams with approval. The glow of the Holy Spirit around them seems to shine with consent. "He has on His robe and on His thigh a name written, KING OF KINGS AND LORD OF LORDS" (Rev. 19:16 NKJV).

When the crowns have been given, following the example of the twenty-four elders, crowns will be placed at Jesus' feet. This is the time of Jesus' coronation. In order to rescue us, Jesus was willing to wear a crown of piercing thorns. His Father is overjoyed now to place the multiple crowns, each increasingly beautiful, on his Son's head. As Revelation 19:12 says, "On His head were many crowns" (NKJV).

We'll all shout and rejoice. Maybe we'll sing "Crown him with many crowns, the Lamb upon his throne." Then we'll stand and sing a heavenly version of the *Hallelujah Chorus*. Wouldn't it be great for the composer Handel to direct us? "The kingdom of the world has become the kingdom of our Lord and of his Christ, and he will reign for ever and ever" (Rev. 11:15).

Finally, I imagine, you will go to your *chupah* and find in your gorgeous home special treasures he has prepared for you. He knows you so well that he created a place, tailor-made for you—and me.

After the marriage ceremony the Jewish groom gave gifts to his bride during their first seven days together (Gen. 34:12). Jesus will give gifts to his bride. Each of us has an individual moment where he lifts our veil and knows our secrets, that deep part of our hearts. He pours out gifts on us: fruit from the Tree of Life, eternal life fully experienced, hidden manna and a white stone, a new name, reigning authority and the Morning Star, white garments, our name in the Book of Life, our name acknowledged before the Father, a position as a pillar of strength, throne privileges, the New Jerusalem—full inheritance. We receive all these gifts because our Bridegroom loves us so much.

Years follow—some think seven years (each year representing a day of earth's time), others think three and one half—of dancing, singing, worshiping, learning, fellowshiping. During our honeymoon, we're well aware of plans for the return mission to planet earth, but before this happens there will be a great banquet.[4]

In the Jewish wedding, the great banquet takes place at the home of the bridegroom, his father's house. We saw earlier that heaven is also called "Father's house." Another name for heaven is the bride, the Lamb's wife (Rev. 21:9). The bride of Christ is so much a part of heaven that she is, in some way, the New Jerusalem; all who go to live there make up the bride. That's a good reason for the marriage supper of the Lamb to take place there. The whole company of heaven comes to the feast of the ages. "Then he said to me, 'Write: "Blessed are those who are called to the marriage supper of the Lamb!"'" (Rev. 19:9 NKJV).

Father God has delighted in making preparations for the feast for His Son. "The Kingdom of Heaven is like a king who prepared a wedding feast for his son" (Matt. 22:1 Jewish New Testament).

King Solomon, who knew how to put on a good banquet said, "He has taken me to the banquet hall, and his banner over me is love" (Song of Songs 2:4).

The Jewish wedding feast has its biggest banquet after the wedding and the seven-day honeymoon. It is likely that our Messiah will follow this pattern. This will be the greatest banquet ever known, and you will be the guest. The wine the Lord will create for the occasion will be the best, assuming that he follows the pattern set by his first public miracle (see John 2:10). What a glorious time we will have.

We will leave the feast strengthened and ready for whatever we are called to do. Angels proclaim that it is time for Jesus' return to earth to set up his kingdom there, too, time to evict Satan and his followers from the earth. (One of the Old Testament names for

God is "Jehovah-Tsabaoth": Lord of the armies of heaven.) Heaven is prepared for this event, and whoever is ready will accompany him for this battle of the ages—perhaps you and I will go! Riding a magnificent white horse, Jesus leads the army, many of whom are on horses also. The multitudes of faithful angels are there in full power.

Those bent on destruction are stopped. You see your Bridegroom now as the Lion of Judah in his victory over evil, and you love him more than ever.

His feet will touch down on the Mount of Olives. With great joy He'll walk down the mountain, through the Golden Gate on the East, and set up his earthly throne in the temple in Jerusalem (Isa. 43:1–5;44:1–2). Finally there will be peace on earth, with King Jesus in charge.

The words of Isaiah foretold the millennial reign of Christ. The animal kingdom will have recovered from the results of humankind's sin and fall from grace: "The wolf also shall dwell with the lamb, and the leopard shall lie down with the kid; ... and a little child shall lead them.... They shall not hurt nor destroy in all my holy mountain: for the earth shall be full of the knowledge of the LORD, as the waters cover the sea" (Isa. 11:6, 9 KJV).

The earth is at total peace, as shown again by Isaiah: "Therefore with joy shall you draw water out of the wells of salvation. And in that day you shall say, Praise the LORD, call upon his name, declare his doings among the people, make mention that his name is exalted. Sing unto the LORD; for he has done excellent things: this is known in all the earth. Cry out and shout, you inhabitants of Zion: for great is the Holy One of Israel in the midst of you" (Isa. 12:3–6 KJV modernized).

Now it's time to do the work King Jesus has given you to do as he reigns on earth. When the time comes, you will know what that work is.

Revelation indicates that at the end of a thousand years, the heavenly city of New Jerusalem will come "down out of heaven from God." (21:2). We may be making trips to heaven and back before this occurs. John saw "a new heaven and a new earth" (v. 1).

The One who "was seated on the throne said, 'I am making everything new!'" (v. 5).

The apostle Peter spoke anointed words in Acts 3:19–21: "Repent, then, and turn to God, so that your sins may be wiped out, that times of refreshing may come from the Lord, and that he may send the Christ, who has been appointed for you—even Jesus. He must remain in heaven until the time comes for God to restore everything, as he promised long ago through his holy prophets."

God will bring restitution of all things from the beginning in Eden to the return of Jesus Christ. We no longer need to weep over the loss of Eden. God has a plan of total restoration, and the end will be better than it was at the beginning. The Lord's Prayer, which the church has faithfully prayed over the centuries, will fully come to pass: God's kingdom will come on earth as it is in heaven. All things will work together for good—forever.

Final Thought

Christians maintain various interpretations of these future events, and your salvation does not depend on how you interpret them. As I said, I've left out a lot. There are more end-time events that I didn't choose to address. When we're there on the spot, we can fill in the missing pieces. Some things just aren't revealed as yet. But here and now we can hold to the hope offered in what has been revealed: "The secret things belong to the LORD our God, but the things revealed belong to us and to our children forever" (Deut. 29:29). Don't forget to study the "Manufacturer's manual," the Bible, to keep yourself ready for the call to come home.

The Bible begins with the creation miracle, the first couple, and their wedding. In the middle is the water-into-wine first miracle of Jesus performed at a wedding. Then the closing miracle, as told in Revelation, takes place at Jesus' own wedding. Thus, we find a trilogy of weddings at the beginning, middle, and end. Three is the signature of God in Scripture, and we see it again here.

The next time you take Communion, as you sip the fruit of the vine, you might, as I do, look up to heaven and say, "Lord, I know you are watching me in my promise of faithfulness to you. I am your betrothed. I am waiting for you, my beloved Lord Jesus.

I am listening for your call to "come up hither.... Rise up, my love ... and come away" (Rev. 4:1 KJV; Song of Solomon 2:10 KJV).

You, the bride, are made of Jews and Gentiles—now one body; races of every color—now one family; churches and messianic synagogues—now one church. All people loving our triune God and loving one another. It is a true love story with the happiest of endings. Alleluia! Alleluia!

CHAPTER FOURTEEN

Ready for Life

All their life in this world . . . had only been the cover and the title page: now at last they were beginning Chapter One of the Great Story, which no one on earth has read: which goes on for ever: in which every chapter is better than the one before.

C. S. Lewis
The Last Battle

My dad, William Harvey Reed, died in 1979, at age eighty-six. He was a short, stocky Scotsman, quite good-looking in his prime. Eventually he became bald, looking like a monk with a half-circle fringe of hair. When he wasn't being too serious about his religious stance, his hazel eyes would twinkle accenting his deep-throated laughter and good sense of humor.

I had the privilege of saying good-bye to him several hours before his death. My brother, Bob, and I stood near Dad's bedside. I had previously learned that a person in a coma can still hear for quite some time. I got close to Dad's left ear, leaned down close, and said clearly, "Dad, when you get to heaven, please give Jesus my love and give Mom my love." Then I prayed, and as I did, he amazed Bob and me both by raising his arms straight in the air, as if to say, "Praise God. All is well."

The night before my father's funeral I received a gift from God, my first poem, which uses very earthly images to tell his story. (Railroad is a primary theme since my grandpa Reed worked for the railroad all his life.)

The Last Train Out

My father had a dream
And in this mystery saw
A train was coming fast.
One that looked so special
'Twas the "last train out."

He had seen many trains
And clackity railroad tracks.
In fact, 'round there was raised.
But this train was different—
Covered with diamonds, rubies, jade.

Each car was more stunning
Than was the one before;
There was such drawing power.
"I mustn't be late," he thought,
"It is the last train out."

The train pulled up and stopped.
Four children gathered 'round
To bid him fond farewell.
"All aboard," Conductor cried.
Such joy, yet hard to part.

He got on board that morn.
Lifted his burly arms
To wave good-bye to all.
Found a seat "reserved"
His name engraved in gold.

It was the "last train out";
He was the last child
From his family to catch the train.
'Twas the last one to leave;
Left promptly, 3:30 A.M.

He decided to take a walk
To see what the train was like;
He met old friends and new.
Had such a splendid time
All sadness was gone for good.

Train smoothly glided in
To a station of pure gold.
Oh, what a sight to view!
Dad got off the train,
Walked to the arms of God.

When it comes your turn
To ride the train above,
Don't be surprised to see
Dad Reed there to greet you
His arms lifted in praise.[1]

My dad lived a good, long life, but he'd had a very close call as a young teen. What follows is from the memoirs I recorded shortly before his death; for posterity, he told me many of his significant life experiences. This particular story was meaningful to him and to me. It relates what he remembered of his near drowning in 1906. Unfortunately, he hadn't had the advantage of formal or informal swimming lessons.

Dad's Story

My brother and I took our bicycles and went to the river with my dog, Bruno, who weighed about thirty pounds. It was the St. Claire River between Canada and the United States at Port Huron, Michigan. Mother had told us not to go down to the river, and we had promised her we wouldn't.

But we wound up at the river at the foot of Court Street, right near the train depot. After dropping our bicycles, we got on our tights and started wading around in the water. Neither of us knew how to swim. The only one that knew how was our dog. I was thirteen years old, and my brother, Scott, was fourteen. So we were wading around in the water and kind of swishing around. I had water wings (floating devices) under my arms and decided I'd just go out about three or four feet and then come back.

The river at that point was a mile wide and went as deep as forty feet, with undercurrents. I got out there and tried to get back, but the current was so heavy that, when I turned, one side of the water wing came out from under my arm. I struggled for a few minutes, and then I went under, down near the bottom. I was digging my toes in the sand and knew I was on a slope. I was down about ten feet under water, I'd say.

As I struggled all the air left my lungs. Then I started breathing in water. Every time I took a breath, my lungs got more water in them. I came up once, then I came up twice, and the third time I came up, I thought, *Well, I'm finished*.

I'd been thinking about all the things in my life that I'd done wrong. It just flashed in front of me, and I thought, *Well, I'm going to see Jesus pretty quick!* because I was full of water. Then I went down again.

At one point I saw my dog's feet sticking down through the water. I grabbed hold of one of his feet, but I didn't have strength enough to hang on. He got to going around in a circle where the bubbles were coming up, and at last there weren't any more bubbles going up.

My brother had gone up to the grain elevator and got a boy, probably age sixteen, who happened to be a Christian. He ran two or three hundred feet up to where I was. Seeing Bruno going around in circles, he dived down right under the dog and got hold of me by my hair (I had hair then!) and towed me over. My rescuer wasn't very big, either, but he got me over to the pilings where my brother was, and the two of them pulled me through into shallow water, about three feet deep. Then they dragged me up on the shore, and by that time there were about fifteen or twenty railroad men who came over.

I was lying there full of water. Scott said my tongue was hanging out; my eyes were bulged out. He felt my pulse and couldn't feel any heartbeat. Scott said one of the switchmen had a looking glass in his pocket, and he took it out and put it in front of my mouth, and there was no vapor on it. It showed that I wasn't breathing. They rolled me over a tar barrel that happened to be there—I guess the Lord had it there—and they got all the water out of me they could. Then one of the big switchmen pumped my stomach up and down to see if he could "get something started." The men took turns lifting me up and down, and still my heart hadn't started yet.

Scott was crying. He thought he'd gotten in trouble taking me down there to swim. Another fellow came along and pushed on my stomach. They didn't know anything about the modern way of artificial respiration, never thought of breathing into my mouth or anything. Anyway, they kept at me, shoving me up and down and rolling me around. After about ten or twelve minutes, I guess, maybe more, maybe fifteen, my heart started beating again. That, added to my time in the river, they said, was about twenty minutes.

After a while I woke up and I looked around. First I looked to see if I was in heaven. I saw the boxcars and everything, so I knew I wasn't. I got up unsteadily on my feet and went over to a fellow by the name of McIntosh, a train dispatcher. (He always tried all the brakes and everything on the trains before they started.) I said, "Thank you for saving my life."

He said, "It wasn't me. It was that boy over there. His name is Shirts." So I went over and I put my arm around him and thanked him for saving my life, him and Scott both, and we were all bawling. And my dog was playing around there, licking my feet and hands, because he had been the main helper, that is, outside of the boy who had dived in and got me.

Being without oxygen for ten or fifteen minutes could have caused brain damage, so God must have performed a miracle.

Do Something Now

My dad said, "I'd been thinking about all the things in my life that I'd done wrong. It just flashed in front of me. . . ." I'm so thankful that my dad-to-be had another chance. Fortunately, he made good his commitment to God in his time of distress. In his scrape with death, my father had a review of his life, though he did not have a "near-death experience." Many of those who have NDEs have what has become known as a "life review."

Like Craig Gottschalk, Carolyn McCormick, and Deborah O'Donnell, many "walk" through life's scenario from beginning to the end. Craig said, "It is said that when people die, their life flashes before their eyes; they see their whole lives in panoramic view. . . . It is exactly what happened to me. My life was played back for me to watch like a video. Every sin I had committed from childhood to the time I was eighteen had been recorded and now was being played back." (Remember Craig had not been converted at this time.)

And Carolyn said, "In a realm in which time seemed nonexistent, I was allowed to start my life over. Events were chronological, but time didn't exist. I reexperienced my whole life. It wasn't as if I saw my life or was told about it; I was there. I 'relived' the same feelings and the same experiences, but this time I was in two places at once. I was a baby or a toddler and was also aware of myself as an adult 'looking on' with an angel."

Deborah's review came at her return. "As life came back to me, my earthly memory bank returned. I now relived that experience—not as one observing from the outside. . . . I was an infant in the incubator. . . . Then I was in my crib playing with my toys. Next I was three years old."

My father and Craig, Carolyn, and Deborah did nothing intentional to review their lives. But each of us—whether or not we have any reason to believe that death is imminent—can choose to allow God to walk with us through our past, to reveal hurts, pains, and scars and to heal them. A foretaste of the healing touch of heaven can be ours here on earth. Speaking of the New Jerusalem, John says, "He will wipe every tear from their eyes. There will be no more death or mourning or crying or pain" (Rev. 21:4). That promise isn't fulfilled here and now, but Jesus, speaking of this life, did say, "I have come that they may have life, and have it to the full" (John 10:10). Abundant, victorious life!

Many of us are heavy laden with the weight of what some might call "unfinished business"—memories that bruise us emotionally and then fester for years, relationships that are not reconciled, chronic thoughts that haunt our days and nights, losses that have not been dealt with. Christ wants to heal our wounds, free us from our fetters, bring light into the dark corners of our lives.

The psalmist David said, "Search me, O God, and know my heart"(Ps. 139:23). To search the heart means to have an intensive review. Only God knows your heart, and he will gently reveal what areas need his cure. Your heart (Gk. *kardia*) is the center of your soul just as your physical heart is the center of your body. God wants to heal the heart's deep emotions and memories (Ps. 26:2). He will do the searching, but you have to be willing to open the eyes of your heart and let his light come in. Let me show you how this worked with my friend Judy.

In October 1995 I met Judy Brown, a forty-seven-year-old widow. She had been watching a show I host at Trinity Broadcasting Network. She called the studio to speak with one of my interviewees: my pastor's wife and a Christian therapist, Betsy McConnell. Betsy introduced me to Judy and her story.

As a young woman, Judy had launched a career in fashion design. For two years she had been happily married to Don, an opera singer and university professor. But tragedy struck when her husband choked to death on a piece of meat when he was eating while alone at home. Realizing she wouldn't have known what to do to help him even if she had been there, she changed careers, entering the nursing profession.

Suffering from years of environmental illness, Judy was now bedridden and housebound, living with her mother, Elayne. She had experienced much trauma in her life, and despite intensive counseling for twenty years, she still had many tormenting memories. Judy was asking Betsy for counsel. Various details, including the fact that Judy lived two hours away and could not travel, seemed like a big order even for a trained therapist. Betsy asked what I thought she should do. Would I join her in this mission? I said yes. And I'm so happy I did. We found Judy to be an attractive, petite woman with shoulder-length brunette hair. Judy was a jewel of a person. She had been a frequent viewer of the show I hosted, and she was thrilled that I would come to see her. And I in turn was inspired by Judy as I walked with her in a year-long journey. On two occasions Betsy and I visited Judy's home together. A third time I visited with another prayer-team member.[2]

We talked and prayed. It was wonderful praying with Judy because she was so ready and open to God's grace. She was ready to allow the light of Christ to shine in to the dark corners of her life. We would stay about three hours, and each time we were there, a major miracle would occur along with some smaller ones. During our first visit Judy was released from a twenty-year-long death wish—daily thoughts of wanting to die. At our next visit she received healing of wounded memories from her father's suicide, and she was able to enter into a closer relationship with her mother. At our third session she was healed of memories that prompted longstanding guilt, and she was able to let go of the pain caused by the death of a close friend.

Between trips, Betsy continued as her counselor by phone, and I took the role of a prayer partner by phone. Judy ordered many healing books and tapes from my ministry, Christian Renewal Association. Following our meetings she wrote, "Because of your [team's] ministry there is a quiet, peaceful place deep inside of me, free of anger and full of love. That has been my greatest gift in this lifetime. God saved the best for last. Isn't that just like Him?"

Judy suspected she had cancer, which was eventually diagnosed by a doctor who was willing to make a home visit. The prognosis was not good, and going to the hospital would likely cause immediate death due to her environmental sensitivities, so Judy's mother, also a nurse, along with her sister, Lynette, took up her physical care. Thus began the big challenge of facing death.

When I finished writing the first nine chapters of this book, I asked Judy if she would like to read them. She said she had been hoping I would ask. Her handwritten comments in the margins were encouraging and helpful. We then talked on the phone about heaven many times, and I answered questions as I could or found the answers. I read to her about the glories of heaven and then would pray with her. It was wonderful to be able to talk so openly about things to come.

We never discounted the knowledge that she could be healed supernaturally. But if that didn't happen, we knew she should be prepared to make her final journey. When Judy got so weak that she could hardly speak, I read her the words from Joni Eareckson Tada's book *Heaven*, "The faintest prayers of those who suffer reach more deeply into God's heart."

She whispered, "Oh that's good to hear." She—and Joni—understood what a great physical and emotional effort it takes for a suffering person to utter a prayer. God applauds this act of love.

During Judy's illness she continued to minister to others in many ways: writing to prisoners, giving financial gifts to worthy causes, and sending videotapes to help friends. In her weakness she was leading family members and friends to God or closer to him. He gave her supernatural strength at those times when she shared her faith. Her voice would be strong momentarily, and then it would fade when the message or exhortation was completed.

When the time of her departure neared, I shared reflective thoughts with her and then prayed. "Judy, like a baby being born, you're going to slip out of this world into the next. You'll step out of your body, like taking off old, but dear, clothes. You'll be back for them at the resurrection. But it's not that they'll have been repaired; they'll have been totally renovated cell by cell. It's better than the fountain of youth; you'll be at the prime age of your life. Soon you'll be seeing family members on the other side, especially your beloved husband, Don."

Or I'd pray, "Dear Father, please comfort your child at this very difficult time of her passing from this life to the greater life. And Jesus, please take her pain. You know what pain is like, for you suffered excruciating pain from the cruelty of humankind and a torturous death on the cross. It's your desire to bear her burden with her. Please carry what she cannot handle. Abba, Father, her times are in your hands. You know just how many days she has left. I know she wants each day to be used for the maximum good. Strengthen her for any ministry she has yet to do for others. As did Jesus, may she finish the work you've given her to do (John 17:4). In Jesus' name."

Or I would say, "Soon there will be an angel arriving for you. You'll be carried in his arms to your Father's house. When you get to the glorious sparkling wall and gate of pearl, you'll be so excited to go inside. Jesus will come to meet you and enfold you, a weary traveler, in his healing arms. He'll say, 'Welcome my beloved, my bride. Come into the home I've been preparing for you. I'm so glad you're finally home!'"

Judy's dying process was not lovely. It was very painful, but she always responded to prayer. As Judy faded in and out of a coma, I recommended that her sister, Lynette, read aloud to her some of the

Scriptures I listed in chapter 2. She also read parts of Joni's book. We discussed the fact that people can often hear long after they can express any response; hearing is often the last sense to go.

Near the very end of Judy's life, Lynette and I set up a telephone call. Her family wanted Judy to feel free to leave her shell of a body, which was now beginning to swell with edema. Lynette put the phone to Judy's ear so I could talk to her and pray. This time, Judy could not answer me. As Lynette listened in, I prayed a while. And then it dawned on me that she should get Cambay, Judy's dearly loved, favorite cat, and put him on Judy's bed, placing her hand on him. It was hard for her to leave her special four-legged friend. I told Judy that it was okay for her to leave Cambay. He would miss her greatly, but her mother, Elayne, loved him and he would be okay.

Shortly before our conversation, I had come across some of Paul's last recorded words, which I read to Judy: "For I am now ready to be offered, and the time of my departure is at hand. I have fought a good fight, I have finished my course, I have kept the faith" (2 Tim. 4:6–7 KJV).

Then I remembered the words of Simeon, an old man facing death: "Lord, now let your servant depart in peace, according to your word" (Luke 2:29 KJV modernized).

And Jesus' last words from the cross: "Father, into your hands I commend my spirit" (Luke 23:46 KJV modernized).

I drew on these Scriptures in my last prayer with her: "Father, I know Judy has kept the faith; she's fought a good fight and finished her work. May her spirit depart in peace, as your Word says. Watch over her in these last days or hours. Send your angels to minister to her, to assist and comfort her. Help her know how very much you love her and how much we all love her. Surround her with healing love and light. She has done everything to prepare for her journey. Help her know that it's okay for her to leave her family and friends. I release her into your care. Into your hands, dear Father, I commend Judy's spirit. In Jesus' name."

Judy died in her sleep a day and a half later, September 24, 1996, 8:45 A.M. Those who saw her at the end were surprised to see that she died with a smile on her face. Elayne said, "I feel as if every cell of my body is sobbing. I just can't stop crying; part of my soul and body is gone. The only thing that comforts me is that she's at peace and that we'll meet again on Resurrection day." As Judy's family grieved her loss, I reminded Elayne that tears and grief mean we loved a lot. Losing a daughter is like losing a part of the mother's own body. The pain is tremendous. The two hardest losses are those of a mate and of a child. The death of someone close hurts so deeply because we know it will never be quite the same without this loved one.

God's caring ways and timing are amazing. He set up our meeting knowing that I would be writing about heaven and therefore be more ready than ever to help one of his choice daughters on her way home. It was such a privilege for me to be a part of Judy's life and death. During our year of sharing she became a close friend.

I encourage you to do your own life review now. That is, work on those hurts that are still bothering you. You can be set free. God has answers for your emotional needs just as he had for Judy. Though a fine Christian for years, without emotional healing she would not have gone through her last year as victoriously as she did. She told me this many times. She needed to unload the emotional pain so she could cope with the physical pain. Though her body was wasting away, her spirit and soul were at peace and rejoicing within.

Encouraging Someone Who Is Facing Death

From Judy's story I want to make another point, addressed especially to people who are caring for someone who is dying. When someone is very ill, don't park him or her in front of the television to make it easy, so neither one of you has to talk about "difficult" topics. There are of course some good programs to watch. Judy found Christian television invaluable, especially since she was housebound. It was a gift to her; the people she watched became her friends. But there is no substitute for *talking*.

Terminally ill people need to talk about their losses, about where they are going, about the life to come, about who will take care of special treasures left behind. Perhaps they need to confess some memories or sins that are still troublesome. It is important that you help them or find someone who can. Be prepared to read aloud healing Scriptures and books. It can be a time of spiritual growth for everyone. Be sure to watch for—and name—the little miracles God performs at such times. You can be a part of the blessing.

Your Life Review

Judy had searched her heart and reconciled with everyone before her death. She had time for an intensive review, and no doubt you have time to do a life review now.

The bottom line for a life review now is being a 100 percent forgiver. An overcomer is a forgiver. We can't run the race effectively without seriously working in this area throughout life. And since no unforgiveness can enter heaven, we must take care of it here. The "wood, hay, and stubble" will be burned. Carolyn's experience gives us a glimpse of how God might deal with this. God's angel lovingly worked with Carolyn, releasing her. At heaven's gates, the angel will want to know: Have you forgiven, or are you willing to forgive everyone? In his book *The Great Divorce*, C. S. Lewis depicts some "unforgivers" being met in heaven by the very people they begrudged. Still being unwilling to forgive, they chose not to enter the gates.

My recommendation is that you do your forgiveness work now. Not only will it help you at death, it will help you in life. You will be a happier, healthier, more effective person in your present life. Forgiving everyone seems like a tall order, especially if you've lived many years and not taken God's admonition seriously. You may do this alone, but I recommend having a prayer partner. Where does one begin? If no one you need to forgive comes immediately to mind, think back to your formative years—to your parents. Did you feel loved by one or both of them? If not, what took that love away? Is there someone to forgive? If so, review that memory being sure to appropriate the knowledge that God loves you unreservedly and that he has always been with you even though you may not have known it then. For assurance of God's unconditional love read John 3:16, and for assurance of God's omnipresence read Psalm 139. Pray through the memory, acknowledging Jesus' healing presence in every hurtful place. When the memory is healed, write down what the Holy Spirit says to you. Speak forgiveness from that span of time. If you were nine years old, then let that nine-year-old part of you forgive.

Deborah O'Donnell said in her life review, "My memories, mixed with awareness of God's omnipresence, gave me peace." Awareness of God's omnipresence is very healing.

Remember how Carolyn McCormick, who was unhappy as a child, said to God, "Living on earth is so painful; there can't be any meaning for it"? The angel took her through all the hurtful experiences of her life and explained the reasons why things had happened and the benefits derived from them. She had been angry at God, her parents, siblings, and a number of other people. Carolyn said further, "But now I was able to forgive those who had injured me or who I thought had injured me."

Those are steps you, too, can take in prayer. As you do, you will see how eventually your whole life will be reconciled from the beginning right up to your present moment. It may take you five or six months to do this as it did with Judy Brown (on a bi-monthly basis, in this case), or possibly longer.

You could pray through your whole life in five-year increments as my friend Shirley Wilson did some years ago. Note each time you feel released and healed to forgive; journal these times of prayer to remind you of your victories and insights given you.

Though most hurts deal with others' sins against you, you may see that your reactions have been sinful too. If you belong to a sacramental church, you may want to confess your sins to God with your minister's guidance. Ministers of all denominations can pray with you and offer counsel. Our own sins wound us, even as do others' sins against us.

I also recommend that you get into a good Bible study. The Word of God heals as does prayer. These two are a winning combination. As you study, look for applications for your life. Make it your life's goal to study the entire Bible in detail. (Be sure you study with those who are trained to do this effectively.) This is the best gift you can give yourself. Because life is so busy, a weekly commitment to a group will help keep this as a top priority.

In summary, consider these questions:

1. Have you prayerfully looked at your relationships?
2. Do you have memories that are still painful? Have you prayed through them, appropriating God's unconditional love and omnipresence?
3. Have you forgiven parents, parent figures, siblings, mate, children, ancestors, neighbors, others?
4. Do you need someone to help you with this process?
5. Are you in a Bible study and growing in understanding? Is God speaking to you through his Word?
6. Are you journaling what you're learning?
7. Have you found a church home?

If you're willing to be a 100 percent forgiver, you're saying to God, "Search me, O God, and know my heart; test me and know my anxious thoughts. See if there is any offensive way in me, and lead me in the way everlasting" (Ps. 139:23 NIV).

> *Test me, O LORD, and try me,*
> *examine my heart and my mind;*
> *for your love is ever before me,*
> *and I walk continually in your truth.*
> (Ps. 26:2–3)

Doing these things will lead you to victorious Christian living.

Walking Through Loss and Grief

I wasn't always as brave as Judy and her family, nor did I know what to do when I first heard thunder in the distance—Dennis's heart condition—warning me of my own possible loss. Before Dennis died in 1991 I had not heard teaching on death and dying and how to cope with it. That is usually left to the bereavement counselors after the fact.

Aware of my husband's progressive heart condition, I once asked a recently widowed woman how she was doing. Her answer:

"Everything is just fine." A short time later I talked to another widow, who gave a similar answer. Nobody would talk. I wish they had confided, "It hurts. I'm in pain. This is what I've found help-ful. . . ." I needed honest sharing.

After Dennis died I went to a local boutique and there saw a clerk, a widow of some twenty years. I thought, *She certainly will have a helpful word for me; after all these years she must be doing well. She's remarried now; she's made a new life.*

I went up to her and said, "I guess we've got something in com-mon now since I recently lost my husband." To my surprise her eyes teared up as she said, "Excuse me" and quickly walked away. I wan-dered around the store looking at merchandise, feeling slightly embarrassed. I wondered what I had done wrong. After about ten minutes my acquaintance came back and said, "Well, I could give you a hug." The hug I received gratefully. With no further conversa-tion she left to help other customers. What did I need back then? I was looking for someone who had been through the same loss and could say, "It's going to be all right. I've made it, and you can too."

Later I thought back about that dear woman and realized that time in itself is not a guarantee of healing; this businesswoman was still unhealed after twenty years. But in less than two years I was healed through emotional healing prayer, and the *rhema* (personal word) of Scripture, and personal testimonies—mostly in books. My joy is that I now am enabled to help the bereaved receive God's healing. This is one evidence of the way God can work "everything together for good."

If you've lost a loved one to death, maybe you're not through the woods yet. As I said earlier, I found praying about my last day with Dennis an important key. This is especially true if you didn't have a chance to say good-bye.

Norma Breiwick lost her fifty-three-year-old husband, Rod-ney, on Monday, August 5, 1996. He died of a heart attack, and she had no real chance for proper good-byes, either. When I met her five weeks later, on September 19, she was medicated for insom-nia and depression, but it just wasn't helping.

Norma said later, "I had not slept or eaten much for three weeks. Getting weaker every day, I was headed for a breakdown.

I was losing hope and felt like giving up. I couldn't shed a tear. My whole back ached and was so heavy it felt ready to collapse. The muscles in my shoulders and jaw were extremely tight and painful. I really didn't want to be at the Christian Renewal meeting, but I came because a dear friend called and told me that I had to be at that meeting no matter what."

Our small prayer group gathered around Norma as she told her story about her last day with Rodney. "On Sunday I had gone to church alone because Rodney had a headache. Then I'd gone to lunch with girlfriends. Arriving home, I found Rodney watching the closing ceremony of the Olympic games. He was in good spirits, telling me things I'd missed on the show.

"Then he asked me if I'd prepare a lamb dinner, which I did: lamb chops, potatoes, and corn. We had a happy evening together. And then at 5:30 A.M., the next morning, he awakened with a severe headache; he got up for an icepack and asked me to rub his chest because of pain there. He was sweating so much, I was drying his head and face while rubbing his chest. When I looked at his face, I knew it was time to call 911. Someone on the phone talked me through artificial respiration techniques until the paramedics arrived. Before 6:00 A.M. Rodney was pronounced dead."

I validated Norma's pain from the sudden death of her husband, which had left little time for closure. Norma then said how guilty she felt about having gone out to eat and not coming straight home. Of course, on a regular day this situation would not have prompted regrets. It's just that Norma didn't know it would be their last day.

We prayed about that last Sunday together, asking the Holy Spirit to reveal a particular time and place at which she could be assured of Jesus' presence. Thinking of the dinner scene, Norma invited Jesus to show his presence. As the group interceded, she was aware of his presence there at their table. Through prayer, it was revealed that the lamb, which Rodney had requested, could represent the Old Testament Passover Feast and its fulfillment in the New Testament Lord's Supper—the Last Supper. We realized that Jesus, the Lamb of God, wanted her to know he was there at their last supper together. The meal took on new meaning as Norma accepted this new awareness of Christ's gracing presence.

Norma was then able to ask Jesus, her Mediator, to tell Rodney, now in heaven, "good-bye," and that she loved him and would miss him greatly. Great sobs were released from Norma for about ten minutes following the prayer. The group gathered closer around her and held her. During this prayer God reassured her that both she and her husband were in his care. With a big smile and tears, Norma said, "The shoulder pain and weight on my back has left me, instantly." We all rejoiced with her. A month later when our prayer group met again, Norma was radiant as she told how well she was doing. She had begun to sleep again that very night.

God is the Healer; we were his vessels. There may be other memories for Norma to work through, but the deepest hurt—the regret regarding events immediately preceding Rodney's death— was healed. Each person's healing timetable is different.

Grief is your personal response to loss. For Norma, her tears released good grief, healing grief. It is important not to advise a bereaved person to stop grieving. Crying and talking can help to uncork bottled-up grief-causing depression. Shakespeare knew the importance of expressing pain. In *Macbeth* he wrote, "Give sorrow words: The grief that does not speak whispers the o'er-frought heart and bids it break."

Yet crying and talking without accompanying prayer is incomplete. Prayer—prayer that reaches deep into the heart to release the pain—is where the healing takes place. If you find praying by yourself isn't healing for you, try to find a small compassionate prayer group or team to help you. Jesus put it this way: "If two of you shall agree on earth as touching any thing that they shall ask, it shall be done for them by my Father who is in heaven. For where two or three are gathered together in my name, there am I in the midst of them" (Matt. 18:19–20 KJV).

We who know God do not need to "grieve like the rest of men, who have no hope" (1 Thess. 4:13). And yet Jesus himself in the Sermon on the Mount said, "Blessed are those who mourn, for they will be comforted" (Matt. 5:4). Mourning is grief that is expressed in front of others. And others can help us as we walk toward recovery. God's desire eventually is complete healing. Isaiah prophetically describes Jesus as the One who came to "bind up the brokenhearted" (61:1), "to comfort all that mourn" (v. 2). That's what he did for Norma, for me, and for multitudes of others.

Two special *rhema* Scriptures were given to me while I was in my own grief. ". . . Your days of sorrow will end," and "As one whom his mother comforts, so will I comfort you; and you shall be comforted in Jerusalem" (Isa. 60:20; 66:13 NKJV). Both of these Scriptures came to pass, and, true to this word, I was comforted, literally, in Jerusalem.

You can tell that your healing is not complete if you are still going over the if onlys, the should haves, and the ought to haves; if you've lost aliveness and spontaneity; if you can't feel God's presence as you used to; if meaning and purpose in life are gone; if you haven't been reconciled with your past; and if you can't praise God in your soul's emotions even though you know your spirit is rejoicing. This takes time and cannot be rushed.

I recommend journaling your pain and your victory; writing and articulating your thoughts is a healing activity. Through your struggles you will grow. You will mature in Christ. You will become a stronger person. By God's grace, you will come out of the woods and into the clearing. Then he can give you a vision of his plans for your future. He has a purpose for you being here and will direct your pathway.

Don't Fear the D Word

Many people fear the *D* word. I know I used to be that way, though not as extreme as some, who will not attend funerals or wakes. It was not a subject I was comfortable talking about. I have to admit that I prefer talking about life, but I can now be comfortable either way. My joy is in talking about that which helps and strengthens others.

Though Judy didn't know me until I was healed from my grief, she did see an earlier videotape of me talking about overcoming grief. She noted a clear difference in my countenance now as opposed to then. As I look at photographs taken during my period of bereavement, I can see a mask of grief that is now gone.

Peter Clarke, senior lecturer in History and Sociology of Religion at King's College, University of London, said, "To refuse to contemplate death, to put it to one side, to hide from it, to live in fear of it, is to destroy the chance of obtaining the wholeness for which a person is born."[3] And as a widow, the late Catherine Marshall said, "Only when one is no longer afraid to die, is one no longer afraid at all."[4]

Until I looked death in the face when Dennis died, I had not come to terms with death—"that imposter," as Shakespeare called it, or in the words of the apostle Paul, "the last enemy to be destroyed" (1 Cor. 15:26). Later in the same chapter, Paul, reflecting on Jesus' resurrection, gives the famous victor's cry, "'Death is swallowed up in victory. O Death, where is your sting? O Hades, where is your victory?' ... But thanks be to God, who gives us the victory through our Lord Jesus Christ" (vv. 15:54–57 NKJV).

The men and women who told their stories in part 2 of this book have made the witness that they are not afraid to die again when their time comes. They have received a gift—lack of fear—that no one can take away from them. I have had the assurance for many years that my salvation is secure; even so, I used to be somewhat afraid to go alone into a dark house. Not any more. Now I think, *Dennis has completed the hardest of human experiences— dying. Why should I be afraid of the unknown of a dark house or anything else, even death?*

But I should warn you, having no fear of death does not mean that one has a license to take a shortcut out of this life. God is a God of mercy, but it is too dangerous a risk to even consider suicide as a way out. Eternity in the wrong place is a long, long time. If you're thinking of ending your own life, seek help. There are answers for you.[5]

Life or Death, Don't Take a Chance

We don't know what will happen in the last microseconds of a nonbeliever's life. Perhaps he or she will be able to say yes to Jesus. But whoever dies without receiving the Savior will be resurrected to stand at the Great White Throne for a life review. Then it will be too late. That person will not have a "reserved seat" in heaven.

I am reminded of a classic quote known as "Pascal's Wager." The issues here are life or death: "Let us weigh the gain and the loss in wagering that God is. Let us estimate these two chances. If you gain, you gain all; if you lose, you lose nothing. Wager then without hesitation that He is." If we wager that He is not, and He is, we have lost everything. If we wager that He is, and there is no life beyond this life, we have lost nothing. Blaise Pascal was certainly right simply from the aspect of logic.

I like to ask those who want to believe but don't know how, to pray what I call the "If" prayer:

> Father God, if you exist, and if you have a Son named Jesus Christ; if he loved me so much that he came all the way from heaven to pay the penalty for my sin by dying in my place, cleansing me and making me God's child; if Jesus actually rose from the grave and ascended into heaven; if he sent the Holy Spirit to live in me, making that most important connection between earth and heaven, then I ask you, Jesus Christ, to mend my brokenness, wash away my sin, and come into my inner being, my spirit, right now. Save my soul. Reveal yourself to me, Lord Jesus, as God incarnate—the One who put on human flesh, the one who came to give me everlasting life and assurance of heaven. In Jesus' name I pray. Amen.

Pray that prayer out loud, slowly, just as it is. When you feel comfortable, pray it again, leaving out the "ifs." Take time to confess any specific wrongdoing, resolving to make amends where possible. Tell someone what you have done. Jesus says that when you confess him before others, he will then confess you before his Father in heaven (Matt. 10:32–33). We who know Him are experiencing the beginnings of heaven on earth. The greatest evidence of this is our changed lives.

Maybe you couldn't pray the prayer at all. Try it again in a month, and again later. If you still can't pray it, do me a favor. In that last microsecond when you are dying and you see Jesus and his amazing light, immediately fall at his feet and ask his forgiveness for your sins. Tell him you want to be his friend and confess Jesus Christ as your Lord and King. I wish you wouldn't wait that long, because you're cutting it far too close, but I hope you'll make it.

Valvita Jones experienced Jesus as the bridge, the way, between earth and heaven. She said, "I will never forget this as long as I live. When Christ had stepped away from me, he turned sideways and stretched out his arms as a bridge. One arm extended to me and one to the Father. His arms were extended as if they were making a cross and a bridge to cross over."

The reason Jesus came to earth was to bridge this gap, this chasm, for Valvita, and for you and me. His purpose was to put heaven into us and to bring us to heaven. If you walked across the bridge of faith holding his hand, you are experiencing the beginning of heaven right now.

In this book you've seen a number of pictures of heaven. One with a person entering heaven individually. Another with people entering heaven en masse. Now here's a little snapshot of heaven for you to easily look at, or to give a friend who might need it.

A Snapshot for You

Heaven is twofold. It is first of all within, and then in the universe. Heaven above is on at least an eleventh dimension, or beyond dimension, so the actual location isn't something we can even comprehend. It's in outer space, perhaps even in another universe. Heaven is the home—an actual place—prepared for all who love God and His son, Jesus Christ. The Creator of the universe has invited us into His family. (That was the purpose for our being on planet earth from the beginning.) Heaven is a place where people love one another and do not say and do unkind things. It's a healing place where you experience complete fulfilment.

The buildings are of made of gold, silver, and precious stones. They are elegant, brilliant, and beautiful. The New Jerusalem will be a bit like earthly Jerusalem with the throne room at its center and walls and gates surrounding it. We've seen how gloriously the jasper walls are decorated, with a rainbow of twelve kinds of precious stones. The throne of God—connecting earth and heaven—is far beyond anything we've seen on earth.

As you pass the sparkling walls and enter the inviting pearl gate, there is a golden boulevard on either side of a beautiful river of life that ripples and flows with vitality. There are trees of life,with twelve kinds of fruit, growing on either side of this river.

Our senses of sight and smell are nearly overwhelmed by heaven. Everything is full of light. The light comes from the glory of God, which has the most beautiful glow imaginable, and the transparent streets of gold add to the radiance. There are parks as beautiful as the Garden of Eden itself and at least one mountain we know of (Rev. 21:10). The fragrances of roses and lilies of the valley are there, emanating from Christ's presence. At times His fragrance is like frankincense, aloes, and cassia. The elders around the throne also have golden vials of incense that are the prayers of the saints that were collected from earth. The fragrance of the flowers in the parks is carried by the gentle breeze.

Music is everywhere. Angels are singing God's praises, people are singing songs of joy, and Jesus sings of His love for us. All are praising God with the words "Holy, Holy, Holy is the Lord." Angels are everywhere worshiping God and rejoicing; they're so glad we "made it" into the Kingdom. Everyone will be able to sing beautifully in ranges far exceeding anything ever heard or sung on earth. The elders around the throne will produce music on their harps and sing praise songs (Rev. 5:8–9).

And there is dancing—even as King David danced before the Lord on earth, so he and multitudes of us will dance in heaven. The once-prodigal son will also be there, dancing. We will share in a different kind of party—God's party. Those who do not want to be happy, loving, and kind will not be invited. Heaven is a place of total unity, healing, and love.

We have become saints, purified and holy. Our garments are white and spotless. No more can temptations of the world contaminate our minds, souls, and bodies. There is no need to battle the weakness of the flesh. We've finished the race and won.

And we can trust everyone because we all want the best for each other. This is a place of friendship and fellowship. All are best friends.

We will enjoy learning because this is a place of the highest wisdom. There is no end to God's omniscient knowledge. He will be our teacher, and perhaps those He designates will assist. We'll plumb the depths of His truths and understand more about His written Word than we ever could on earth. We'll be taught about the universe by the Creator Himself.

We'll grow from "grace to grace, from glory to glory," living in His presence, growing into the maturity and likeness of Jesus our Savior, Husband, and King. And growing to be like our dear and glorious Abba, Father. All this in the power of the Holy Spirit.

We'll also be taught how to be true leaders and the kings He's called us to be. This will be a time of preparation for the great plans of the ages that God will reveal to us. The adventure with God will never end.

Ready for Life

Here in these pages, you have looked at seven inspiring people touched by heaven: Valvita, Deborah, Gerard, Caroline, Pam, Lorraine, and Craig. Their stories have encouraged and uplifted you. You've heard from some of the people in antiquity who saw heaven and described it: Ezekiel, Isaiah, Moses, the apostle Paul, and the apostle and revelator John. Here in this chapter you have seen how others have been healed to live victorious lives or to complete their journeys home. A number of times in the book you've been lifted up on tiptoe to take a peek at the other side. From that vantage point, you have perhaps begun to find meaning for everything that has happened during your life. Heaven's perspective heals the soul. Let me conclude with an example of this.

On November 1, earlier in the afternoon that Dennis died, he called me on our intercom and said with excitement in his voice, "Rita, meet me in the kitchen. I have a letter I want to show you."

My response was, "Yes, Denny, I'll be right there." As I left my office and walked down the hall, I wondered at his request. Dennis had never asked me to come to the kitchen to show me something of importance. This was different. Must be something special.

He was waiting there in front of the window I looked out daily and saw green-topped alder trees lining the hillside. Handing me the letter he said, "This just arrived today from Judy Dupree-Gervais, an Episcopal minister's wife. She's written me before."

I took it and looked at the letter, which was dated October 28. It read:

> Sunday July 14, 1991, the Holy Spirit sent a special prayer for you and Rita . . . and showed me a most holy vision: a great golden light poured down from heaven over the two of you and then flowed out into the world. Then the Lord gave me a message to be sent to you when some money came. . . . I recorded this in my journal and waited for Jesus to send the money, knowing that it would come when he was ready. On October 15, the money did come, but we were leaving for my husband's reunion at his . . . seminary, so I am just now getting this letter off to you and Rita. It is such a joy to deliver this message of God's love to you. . . .
>
> "My light from heaven has poured down upon you and will flood you still more, that you will have abundant strength to finish the work I have given you to do in these last days. You are my beloved, my chosen children whom I love most dearly. Gird yourselves about with my strength, knowing that you will do still greater things for me because I am faithful. I love you. . . ."

What beautiful words. What encouragement. Putting the letter on the counter, I said, "Oh, Denny," and I threw my arms around his neck to give him a big hug. He hugged me back as we stood there filled with love for God and for one another, wondering what it all meant.

We didn't know that would be our last embrace on earth, our last good-bye. How grateful I am for that hug! Oh, that it could have been longer, that I could have said what I needed to say. "I'll never stop loving you. I'll love you forever. I . . ." But that will have to be for another time, for a better place.

It took time, many months, actually, for me to get heaven's perspective on this message. More encouragement came as I realized the words were for Dennis in heaven and me on earth. Even though Dennis is no longer with us, his ministry continues through his books, teachings and influence. For my part, I have enjoyed amazing strength to carry on the work left behind; friends often comment on this. Only God could help me become a businessperson and accomplish things beyond my natural ability. But Judy was led to get the letter to us just on that day for one reason, thinking she should send us a gift. Her gift was beyond what she ever could have guessed.

I look forward to being with Dennis again in that home prepared for us. While Dennis was my earthly bridegroom, Jesus will be both mine and Dennis's heavenly Bridegroom. I'll get to dance with them both. Maybe we'll all three dance, Hebraic style, hands clasped and in a circle. Then you and others can join us. Now while my heart is focused on heaven, I'm still very active on earth. I'm ready for life.

In this book, you and I have gone to heaven and back together. Heaven has healed some of our earth's sorrows. I trust that you have new zest for living, new hope for your tomorrows, and new vision for what life in the next millennium will bring.

I wish for you also that each day you walk on this earth you will keep listening for the music of heaven, for angel choirs, and choirs of the redeemed. And join me, won't you, for the music I'm especially listening for—a trumpet solo!

Notes

CHAPTER ONE: Looking for Answers

1. "Death Trip," Marvin Barrett, *Lear's* (November 1989), 119.

2. Mally Cox-Chapman, *The Case for Heaven* (New York: G. P. Putnam's Sons, 1995), 2.

3. D. James Kennedy, *Evangelism Explosion*, 4th ed. (Carol Stream, Ill.: Tyndale, 1996), 103.

4. See Sherwin Nuland, *How We Die* (New York: Vintage Books, 1993), 40. He says, "When the brain has been starved of oxygen for longer than the critical two to four minutes, its injury becomes irreversible." Carol Hopkins, nationally registered respiratory therapist and personal friend, relayed in a conversation with me, "One exception to this would be near-drowning in a cold (not icy) lake where people have survived up to twenty-five minutes." She explains further, "It's critical during treatment for them to be warmed up slowly. CPR training gives four to five minutes until death. In a hot climate you have less time, in a cold climate you have more time, and a baby has less time than an adult."

5. Melvin Morse and Paul J. Perry, *Transformed by the Light* (New York: Villard/Random,1992), ix–xiii.

6. Stephen M. Miller, "Back from the Brink," *Physician*, July–August 1995, 8.

7. Melvin Morse and Paul J. Perry, *Closer to the Light* (New York: Ballantine Books, 1990), 202.

8. Ibid., 202–3.

9. Morse and Perry, *Transformed by the Light*, 162.

10. Ibid., 196.

11. Michael B. Sabom, *Recollections of Death* (New York: Harper and Row, 1982), 181.

12. Ibid., 183.

13. *Webster's New Collegiate Dictionary* (Springfield, Mass.: G. & C. Merriam Co., 1979).

14. Susan Blackmore, *Dying to Live* (Amherst, N.Y.: Prometheus Books, 1993), 111.

15. Dennis and Rita Bennett, *Trinity of Man* (Green Forest, Ark.: New Leaf Press, 1987), 98. See this book for a better understanding of the important difference between spirit and soul.

16. Deuteronomy 18:10–12 (NASB): "There shall not be found among you anyone who ... practices witchcraft, or one who interprets omens [fortuneteller], or a sorcerer [does magic through evil spirits], or one who casts a spell [incantation], or a medium, or a spiritist, or one who calls up the dead [by seance or mirror gazing]. For whoever does these things is detestable to the LORD."

17. See Dennis and Rita Bennett, *The Holy Spirit and You* (Brunswick, N.J.: Bridge-Logos, 1971).

18. Quoted in Stephen M. Miller, "Back from the Brink," 8.

19. Finis Jennings Dake, *Dake's Annotated Reference Bible* (Atlanta: Dake Bible Sales), 140; Acts 14:20, n. q.

20. Spiritism is the attempt of human beings to get in contact with the "spirit world," especially with departed relatives and friends, through the help of spirit guides and mediums. This is forbidden in the Bible. When King David's son died, the king said in grief: "I shall go to him, but he shall not return to me" (2 Sam. 12:23 NKJV). This is a safe position to take. God has safety barriers set up between the living and the dead for our protection. We are not to try to bring back spirits of the dead for any reason; to do so is to invite deception and possible demonic oppression or possession.

Occasionally someone reports seeing a dying person's spirit depart. Further seeing of or communication with the departed is forbidden (see 1 Chron. 10:13; Isa. 8:19). Sometimes people claim to see a loved one off and on for a year or more after the loved one's death. Beware of such sightings. Fallen angels have been known to impersonate the departed, causing deception and possible possession. Evil spirits have access to the earth until their judgment (Matt. 8:29; 25:41; Jude 6), but communication with them is forbidden.

21. Over the years I have observed that quite a few authors start well but by their second or third book on the subject of NDEs get off track. Some authors got into reincarnation. Others got into spiritism and communicating with the dead via seances or mirror gazing. Such things are spiritually dangerous and detestable to God (see Deuteronomy 18:9–14).

22. "To Heaven and Back?" Douglas Groothuis, *Christianity Today* (April 1995), 42.

23. First Thessalonians 4:13–18 (NKJV) teaches what some call the Rapture, or catching away, of the church, and verse 18 says to "comfort one another with these words."

CHAPTER TWO: Let Heaven Heal You

1. Rita Bennett, *Inner Wholeness Through the Lord's Prayer* (Grand Rapids: Chosen Books, 1991; reprint, Edmonds, Wash: Christian Renewal Association, 1996).

CHAPTER THREE: Crossing Through His Cross

1. Since 1991 I have been a bimonthly host for the program *Praise Northwest*. This two-hour talk show comes through Trinity Broadcasting Network and their northwest KTBW studio. For a number of years prior to this, my late husband, Dennis, and I had been cohosts on this program.

2. Bernard was a Christian theologian of the Cistercian religious order in Clairvaux, France. He was in charge of a monastery and lived from 1091 to 1153. The quote is attributed to him.

CHAPTER FOUR: I Was in Heaven While My Baby Slept in Her Crib

1. Michael B. Sabom, *Recollections of Death* (New York: Harper and Row, 1982), 212.

CHAPTER FIVE: A Doctor's Story

1. Dr. William Standish Reed founded the Christian Medical Foundation with offices in Tampa, Florida. CMF hosts a yearly Doctor's Conference of Logos Psychosomatic Medicine.

2. When Jesus heard the news that his good friend Lazarus was very ill, he said, "This sickness is not unto death, but it happened to bring glory to God. It will be the means by which Jesus, the Son of God, will receive glory" (John 11:4, my paraphrase). Likewise, every word in this testimony is for the glory of God and his Son Jesus.

3. Denise said, "Later I thought about 1 John 1:9. I remembered that if we earnestly confess our sins, then God forgives us and the blood of Jesus Christ cleanses us from all unrighteousness."

4. Quotation source unknown.

5. Hospital Christian Fellowship is an organization of Christian care-givers, founded in 1936. HCF is active in 100 countries and its headquarters is in South Africa. Calvary Commission is headquartered in Lindale, Texas, and was founded in 1978 by the Reverend Joe Fauss. This is a ministry to reach prisoners with the Good News. Calvary is now reaching out to four other nations—India, Romania, Belize, and Mexico.

CHAPTER SIX: From Moths to Butterflies

1. The conference was under the auspices of the Episcopal Diocese of Oregon. Dr. Liz Glover was the convener.

CHAPTER EIGHT: Escape from the River of Death

1. The Reverend Ruben Korpi was pastor four years at Church by the Side of the Road in Seattle, Washington, as well as at many other churches during his fifty years of ministry. He is now retired and living in Yelm, Washington, with his wife, Betty. They are a musical team and are still active in ministry.

2. See Revelation 21:17–20.

3. Paul H. Tutmarc Sr., deceased, was a professional musician and the inventor of the electric guitar in 1931 and the electric bass in 1933. His son, Paul H. Tutmarc Jr. (Bud), continues with the legacy received from his father, play-

ing the Hawaiian steel guitar. This he does in many parts of the world. Bud's albums have been released in Europe through WORD, UK, of London, and in Sweden under the PRIM label. He has recorded albums in Mexico City, London, Hawaii, Los Angeles, Nashville, and Seattle. His two latest recordings are *Unforgettables #1* and *Unforgettables #2*. These are recordings of old, favorite love songs and are now released and distributed by Brentwood Music, Inc.

4. Richard Eby, *Caught Up into Paradise* (Old Tappan, N.J.: Fleming H. Revell, 1978), 200–202.

5. Satan, at one time one of God's chief angels, was cast out of heaven—along with other rebellious angels—for mutiny, wanting to take God's place. Though he was defeated and ultimately stripped of his power when Jesus, God incarnate, died to save the human race, he still has a following of rebellious angels (demons) and humans bent on taking as many people as possible with them into destruction.

CHAPTER NINE: Tug-of-War for My Soul

1. See 1 Corinthians 12:3–4 for Paul's experience. Also see Acts 2:17, which says that young men will see visions in the last days.

2. Second Corinthians 5:10: "For we must all appear before the judgment seat of Christ, that each one may receive the things done in the body, according to what he has done, whether good or bad" (NKJV).

3. Revelation 12:10. Scripture calls Satan "the accuser of our brothers, who accuses them before God day and night."

4. Revelation 22:13; see also Psalm 90:2.

5. Craig said, "Later I looked up 'breath' in the Bible, and the word for it in Greek is *pneuma*. Scripture uses *pneuma* for both 'breath' and 'spirit.' In 2 Thessalonians 2:8 the NIV translates *pneuma* as 'breath' and the KJV translates it as 'spirit.' Also in Revelation 11:11 the NIV translates it 'breath' and KJV translates it 'spirit,' so there is a connection between breath and spirit."

CHAPTER TEN: Wonders of the Heavenly City

1. *Cruden's Complete Concordance* (Grand Rapids: Zondervan, 1949), 294–95. This count does not include references to the heavens or heaven meaning the sky or outer space with sun, moon, stars, and planets.

2. Hebrew and Greek meanings from *The New Strong's Exhaustive Concordance of the Bible* (Nashville: Thomas Nelson, 1984), 118, 53.

3. "It is to be noticed that the form of the word (*shamayim*) is neither singular nor plural, but dual. This may be only an ancient form of the plural, but it is supposed by some commentators to imply the existence of a lower and an upper heaven, or of a physical and spiritual heaven—'the heaven and heaven of heavens.'" Robert Baker Girdlestone, Donald R. White, ed. *Synonyms of the Old Testament* (Grand Rapids: Baker, 1983), 267.

4. Dr. Hugh Ross, cited on *Reasons to Believe* TV program, aired on Trinity Broadcasting Network, August 10, 1996. For further information see Hugh Ross, *Beyond the Cosmos* (Colorado Springs: NavPress, 1996).

5. Cited in Henry H. Halley, *Halley's Bible Handbook* (Grand Rapids: Zondervan, 1965), 255.

6. Guy P. Duffield, *Handbook of Bible Lands* (Ventura, Calif.: Regal Books, 1969), 104. Information submitted by Amos Daniel Millard, retired professor of Biblical Archaeology, Northwest College, Kirkland, Washington.

7. Grant R. Jeffrey, *Heaven: The Last Frontier* (Toronto: Frontier Research Publications, 1996), 97.

8. Halley, 608.

9. Names for heaven in the New Testament: the Father's house (John 14:2); a city with foundations (Heb. 11:10); a better country (Heb. 11:15–16); city of the living God (Heb. 12:22); the heavenly Jerusalem (Heb. 12:22); enduring city (Heb. 13:14); the new Jerusalem (Rev. 21:2); the Holy City, Jerusalem (Rev. 21:2, 10; 22:19); the dwelling of God (Rev. 21:3); the bride, the wife of the Lamb (Rev. 21:9).

10. *The Holy Land*, Knopf Guides (New York: Alfred A. Knopf, 1995), 244.

11. Adam Clarke, *Clarke's Commentary*, vol. 5 (Nashville: Abingdon, n.d.), 1059.

12. Matthew Henry, *Matthew Henry's Commentary in One Volume* (Grand Rapids: Zondervan, 1961), 1985.

13. Angels' purposes: Job 38:7; Psalm 34:7; 91:11; Matthew 6:10; 13:41; 18:10; 25:31; Luke 2:9–15; Acts 7:53; Hebrews 2:2; 13:2.

14. Kenneth Copeland and Dr. Carl Baugh, "Understanding Creation" (video series), Kenneth Copeland Ministries, Fort Worth, Texas, 1995.

CHAPTER ELEVEN: Rewards for the Greatest Olympic Game

1. Grant R. Jeffrey, *Heaven: The Last Frontier* (Toronto: Frontier Research Publications, 1990), 165.

2. Adam Clarke, *Clarke's Commentary*, vol 5. (Nashville: Abingdon, n.d.), 239. In the original Clarke mistakenly says that the games were held every fifth year. I have amended it to every fourth year.

3. Merrill F. Unger, R. K. Harrison, ed., *The New Unger's Bible Dictionary* (Chicago: Moody Press, 1985), 456.

4. Dick Mills, *A Good Word for You* publication (Orange, Calif., 1995).

5. Ibid.

6. Clarke, *Commentary*, 5:240.

7. Clarke, *Commentary*, 5:239–40.

8. W. E. Vine, *An Expository Dictionary of New Testament Words* (Old Tappan, N. J.: Revell, 1966), 167.

9. Rita Bennett, *Emotionally Free*® and *Inner Wholeness Through the Lord's Prayer* courses (Edmonds, Wash.: Christian Renewal Publications, 1997).

10. Unger, *New Bible Dictionary*, 822.

11. Cited by Kim Lawton, *Charisma*, October 1995, 54–59.

12. Corrie ten Boom, *The Hiding Place* (Grand Rapids: Revell, 1996), 33.

13. Compiled by Terry Whalin from interviews conducted by various media, "Watch for These Christian Athletes in Atlanta: Profiles of Olympic Athletes," *Charisma*, July 1996, 45–48.

14. Amy Carmichael as quoted in Joni Earickson Tada, *Heaven Your Real Home* (Grand Rapids: Zondervan, 1995), 195.

CHAPTER TWELVE: Heaven's Gifts to Overcomers

1. *The New Strong's Exhaustive Concordance of the Bible* (Greek Dictionary of the New Testament) (Nashville: Thomas Nelson, 1984), 50.

2. Adam Clarke, *Clarke's Commentary* vol. 1 (Nashville: Abingdon, n.d.), 384–85.

3. Ibid., Matthew–Revelation, 5:979.

4. Ibid., 1:983.

5. Bobbi Hromas of American Christian Trust, Rolling Hills, California, was chair of this event.

6. Clarke, *Commentary*, 5:985.

CHAPTER THIRTEEN: Your Heavenly Wedding

1. Joseph Good, *Rosh Hashanah and the Messianic Kingdom to Come* (Port Arthur, Tex.: Hatikva Ministries, 1989), 147.

2. Polly Perkins, *Christ the Bridegroom and Jewish Wedding Customs* (Lynnwood, Wash.: Jewish Christian Ministries 1989), 11.

3. Ibid., 25.

4. Believers may differ on whether it will be held in heaven (New Jerusalem) or on earth (Old Jerusalem). Old Jerusalem is probably not large enough to hold the crowd, whereas heaven can house from 28 billion to 30 trillion people, according to those who have attempted to evaluate it. See Judson Cornwall, *Heaven* (Brunswick, N. J.: Bridge-Logos, 1993), 65.

CHAPTER FOURTEEN: Ready for Life

1. Copyright 1978 Rita Bennett. Revised 1996.

2. Friends Shirley Wilson and Betty Bell, trained in my *Emotionally Free*® course, assisted us as they were able.

3. Peter Clarke, "The Case of New Religions," in *Beyond Death*, Dan Cohn-Sherbok and Christopher Lewis, ed. (New York: St. Martin's Press, 1995), 135.

4. Catherine Marshall, *To Live Again* (Grand Rapids: Chosen Books, 1957, 1969), 86.

5. Rita Bennett, compiler and coauthor, *Suicide Prevention: Understanding and Healing* (Edmonds, Wash.: Christian Renewal Association, 1994).

Recommended Reading

Bramblett, John. *When Good-bye Is Forever: Learning to Live Again After the Loss of a Child.* New York: Ballantine Books, 1991.

A bereaved father's guide to overcoming the tragedy of his child's death. It guides relatives and friends with ways to aid the bereaved.

Cornwall, Judson. *Heaven.* North Brunswick, N.J.: Bridge-Logos, 1989.

Here you will experience comprehensive biblical teaching on heaven by a well-seasoned and treasured pastor.

Eby, Richard. *Caught Up into Paradise.* Old Tappan, N.J.: Revell, 1978.

Dr. Eby tells his life story, beginning with his early childhood and going on through his adult life to the climactic event of his near-death experience.

Jeffrey, Grant R. *Heaven: The Last Frontier.* Toronto: Frontier Research Publications, 1990.

A thorough, well-researched biblical picture of heaven from the catching away of the church to the Second Advent, concluding with a description of the new heaven and earth.

Kreeft, Peter. *Heaven.* San Francisco: Ignatius Press, 1989.

This is the only book on my list that I haven't yet read. I learned about it by reading Joni Eareckson Tada's book *Heaven.* I have been inspired to add it to the list, and I look forward to reading it.

Lewis, C. S. *The Great Divorce.* New York: Macmillan, 1946.

This is a fictional story of a spiritual bus ride from the outskirts of hell to heaven and the reasons why some chose to stay and others chose to leave.

_____. *A Grief Observed.* New York: Macmillan, 1988.

Lewis walks us through the battles he fought to rediscover his faith after the loss of his wife. This masterpiece has comforted thousands.

_____. *The Last Battle.* From the Chronicles of Narnia series. New York: Macmillan, 1956.

This fictional story is the last in the Chronicles of Narnia series. Adventures lead the reader to the realization that the lowly stable is the way into heaven. It concludes with a most beautiful description of God's Country.

Maltz, Betty. *My Glimpse of Eternity.* Grand Rapids: Revell, 1996.

Due to a misdiagnosed burst appendix, Betty dies with peritonitis, glimpses heaven, and is sent back to her husband and family.

Perkins, Polly. *Christ the Bridegroom and Jewish Wedding Customs.* Lynnwood, Wash.: Jewish Christian Ministries, 1989.

This small book is a beautiful resource to help the reader understand the biblical picture of the bride of Christ.

Rawlings, Maurice. *Beyond Death's Door.* Nashville: Nelson, 1978; New York: Bantam, 1979.

Dr. Rawlings, specialist in cardiovascular diseases, is thrust into research on near-death experiences when one of his patients dies and returns with a message. The CPR information at the end of the book is important to know. Though this book may be out of print, it can be obtained through many libraries.

Sabom, Michael B. *Recollections of Death.* New York: Harper and Row, 1982.

Noted cardiologist and professor of Medicine at Emory University, Sabom does a scientific study of the effects of near-death on experiencers. The book is easy reading with interesting stories. It is presently out of print but available in many libraries.

Sauvage, Lester R. *The Open Heart.* Deerfield Beach, Fla.: Health Communications, Inc., 1996.

A world-renowned heart surgeon tells the moving stories of ten of his patients who went to the brink of life and death. Each one came through coronary bypass surgery with renewed purpose in life.

Springer, Rebecca. *Within the Gates*. Dallas: Christ for the Nations, reprinted 1995.

Reasons for the longevity of this seventy-year-old book are revealed when you read about Rebecca's coma and her four-day visit to heaven. When read in small portions at night before retiring, it gives hope to the grieving and works like medication to help them sleep.

Tada, Joni Eareckson. *Heaven: Your Real Home*. Grand Rapids: Zondervan, 1995.

As Joni is an artist on canvas, she is also an artist with words; here she paints a pathway straight to heaven's door.

Wilkerson, Ralph. *Beyond and Back:Those Who Died and Lived to Tell It*. Anaheim, Calif.: Melodyland Productions, 1977.

This biblically oriented book has near-death experiences, near deaths, deaths, and deaths and returns. Pastor for many years, the author does an excellent job relating a wide variety of experiences. This book is out of print but still available in many libraries.